I hope you [like]
this; it's just [something]
which had to be bought for
an old fisherman who should
thrash the water more often.

Happy Christmas Daddy

with all my love,

Pamela

xx

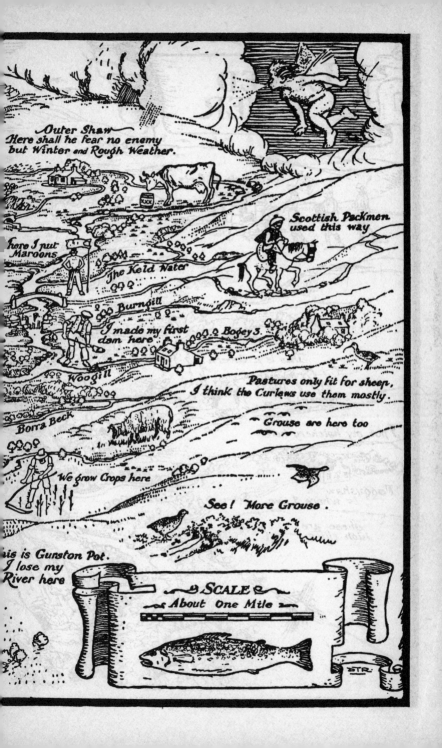

Outer Shaw
Here shall he fear no enemy
but Winter and Rough Weather.

Scottish Packmen
used this way

Here I put
Maroons

The Keld Water

Burngill

I made my first
dam here

Bogey 3.

Woogill

Pastures only fit for sheep,
I think the Curlews use them mostly.

Borra Beck

Grouse are here too

We grow Crops here

See! More Grouse.

This is Gunston Pot.
I lose my
River here

SCALE
About One Mile

Loved River

LOVED RIVER

by

H. R. Jukes

ANDRE DEUTSCH

First published 1935

Reprinted 1984 by André Deutsch Limited
105 Great Russell Street London WC1

Copyright © 1935 by H.R. Jukes
Introduction copyright © 1984 by Antony Atha

ISBN 0 233 97735 X

Printed in Great Britain by
Ebenezer Baylis & Son Limited
The Trinity Press, Worcester and London

Foreword

When I started selecting titles for this series I was given many suggestions by friends and acquaintances. Every fisherman has his favourite fishing book, so the choice of the first eight titles presented little real difficulty. Then, quite independently, two of the leading angling authorities alive today suggested a book that I had never read by an author I had never heard of. I now have read it and here it is as a vindication of their choice.

In many ways it may seem a strange choice at first. For *Loved River* is not about fishing, nor fishing techniques, nor fishing stories, nor advanced fishing instruction, nor even angling entomology. I know nothing of the author except his name, and while I may guess (for there is the odd hint in the text), I do not know the name or whereabouts of the river – the subject of the book. And yet I am sure that it is a classic for it embodies the dream of every angler who has taken rod in hand and wished for the pot of gold at the end of the rainbow. It is the story of a man returning to the river of his childhood and remaking it, fashioning it rather, until he can write on the last page of the book that the river was '. . . at last, the stream that I had dreamed about; the river as I had seen it with the magic eyes of youth. More beautiful, I think, even than that.'

Moreover this was not just a few hundred yards of

some well-tended chalk stream or a famous stretch of salmon river with so-and-so-many holding pools. This was miles, three as the crow flies (according to the author's map), ten, we read in the text, of fishable river and beck, all made and created with loving care and happiness and enjoyment out of an upland limestone stream which had originally a bare half mile of fishable water. The book is the story of how this was done and the adventures that happened along the way. It is there for you to read and it needs no embellishment from me. But there are two fishing anecdotes in this book which I am sure contain a special moral. The first is of the guest whose sights were set so high and whose consequence was so grand that she (for it was a she) was unable to appreciate the beauties and opportunities of the river. Oh, what a revenge was taken on her for her arrogance and her pride.

The second is of the experts, and how, with the help of a few ants' eggs, they were fairly brought to heel. It is perhaps a timely reminder that there are more things in heaven and earth than are dreamt of in any angler's philosophy. No one, however experienced, knows everything and it is always well to stop and listen.

Antony Atha

Contents

*

Chapter I

Scenario

*

You must not think of my river as one of those royal streams whose photographs appear so frequently in all the illustrated weeklies—generally, I have noticed, as a background. No, my river is not like that. Really it is very little wider, and just as winding, just as flower-strewn and fragrant as a little country lane. And just as gossipy. Sometimes, like the road, it encroaches on to the grassy banks, so that you can hardly tell which is grass and which is river; and like the road, too, it has rough places, delightfully rough and bumpy places which create groans or laughter according to your quality as a fisherman or of the car you own. Perhaps you would call it a beck. But it *is* a river; it is marked so on the map.

The map will not show you, however, the details; that is, of course, unless it is a very large map; and it is necessary for the well-being of this book

9

and what you may learn from it, that you should at least know some of them. Let me give you a few of the broader ones, so that you can picture them (or I hope that you may be able to do) as I so often did during the years I was away. For you must know that, until these last few years, I had not seen my river since my boyhood.

First, then, I must tell you that it lies, well-hidden, high up (though not *too* high) among the north-country hills. It has a little valley all its own, exclusively, not like other rivers which join bigger ones and then run off to sea. No, my river is entirely mine, for it actually disappears underground a mile downstream below my house. They say it comes out again a few miles lower down, but I am not interested in that: for me my little dale ends with its river. As a matter of fact it does end almost physically, too; for just where the water, every drop of it, falls bubbling down a dark, wide hole—Gurston Pot, they call it; or they will do in this book, it is near enough—the twin lines of hills which run all round its oval valley like the sides of a rose-bowl, come sweeping in towards each other and suddenly end in two great limestone cliffs which go towering up into the sky, their bases barely a hundred yards apart. The gap between them is closed by trees, high trees, save only where the road, the winding country lane I told you was so like my river, runs like a ribbon through them to my house. So you see we are shut off entirely, like the inmates of a feudal castle with the drawbridge down. I will not take you through the portal yet, because as soon as you are through you will want to linger over details by the wayside; but I will tell you, as I said, the broader outlines. Then, if you still feel that you would like to go, I will guide you through the wood and show you all that I have done.

Four miles upstream, then, there lies across the valley, completely closing it at its head, an important mountain. It must be an important mountain, for, on all the maps, it is coloured in dark brown, and there are not many coloured in as deep a tone as that. In fact it must be one of the biggest that there are. Anyhow it is so big that we can only see a part of it from the valley. It lies there, blocking out the sky, grey-green and smoothly rounded, like the hump of a whale, with the cloud shadows lying blue across it. It is there, from among the springs and peatmosses, that my river takes its birth.

Bounding the valley down its sides run the spurs of lesser hills, some very bold and forward, thrusting out their chests well into the valley; others, more shy, standing back; but all of them with broken, craggy sides where pigeons breed. In places the winds have carved the cliffs into sharp upstanding pinnacles of varying shapes, to which imaginative, sentimental folks have given silly names, such as "My Lady's Candlestick", "The Pope's Nose", and such like follies. At no place will the skylines—that is if you look at them from river-level—be more than a mile apart. At times they will not be more than two or three hundred yards, which makes that part of the valley seem quite a gorge. For a furlong, more or less (everything in my valley is more or less), each side of the stream itself, forming the bottom of the bowl as it were, are flat, lush meadows, which in the summer, though they have the scent of hay, seem to me to grow nothing but blue and purple flowers and yellow wagtails. Then, as the meadows finish, the land lifts quickly up towards the heather, and, above the heather, wild places of benty land and rock where one's blood dances to another music. Pastures there are, of course—"intakes" we call them—but they are all rough and reedy and almost perpendicular. If one walks along them, one foot feels to be a long way below the other. They are only fit for sheep; I think the curlews use them mostly. Then I must not forget to tell you, too, that dotted here and there about the slopes are untrimmed and straggly woods of spruce and birch and hazel, some big, some small,

all lovely: with occasional odd pines which are the loveliest of all. Every ghyll, of course, is clothed with trees, almost to the top, and both banks of my little river are naturally rich with them. From the hilltops, where I will maybe take you soon, if you are still interested, the only way that you can trace its course among the meadows is by the wavy line of trees, for the water only shows occasionally, just here and there where the sun catches it. Then it leaps into view like the sudden flashing of a jewel. The foliage, as one can see, grows sparser towards its head, but even there, where the heather and bracken come sweeping down, even there odd rowans keep popping out in the most delightful, unexpected places. I think the ring ousels—who look like blackbirds with a parson's collar on— must plant them there. That is another place to which, if we are not too busy, I must take you later on. It is a great adventure, or it used to be. But in case we have not time, I will just tell you now that away up there, for that first mile or so through the heather, my river is, it is still, just a little mountain burn.

But here we are, already at the head of the valley, before I have even actually brought you to the fir-wood at its foot. I must get back to the beginning, to the time when I myself came to my valley, not for the first time—for then I should not have been able to describe for you all this from memory—nor for the second, but for the final time.

for the first time.—For then I should not have been

Chapter II

Anticipations

*

I need, of course, not tell you of my journey
north by train. That would be too dull after I
had told you of my river. In any case there are
efficient little strips laid upon all the tables which
keep you sufficiently informed of all the interesting
places you are coming to. They are concise, as they
have to be—one passes through them all so quickly
—and purposely made not too absorbing. The knowledge that there is an inn at Grantham is not sufficiently exciting to keep you awake if you want to
doze: that is unless you are particularly interested in
inns.

I was not interested at all. In fact, now I come to
think of it, I was remarkably calm, considering that
I was being carried towards my river at something
approaching sixty miles per hour. Perhaps the reason
was that I was not going quite straight there. That
would have been too sudden; it would have cut the

delightful time of final anticipations far too short. So I had decided to stay the night in a town which I shall call Furrowfield, more than forty miles away, and to dream, if possible, of the morrow.

But I did not dream. I met some kindred spirits after dinner who were going fishing too, though in a dale a little to the east of mine. They were nice fellows: they talked trout until the early morning.

Chapter III

Up the Fairway

*

The road up the main valley—the valley into
which they say my river comes out again
after it has been underground—is very
beautiful. It is a softer, gentler-looking countryside
than mine, though one can see the hills becoming
bigger at every corner. And my excitement grew
with them too, for with each one I remembered
more. Broad outlines gave place to little details,
and I could hardly restrain myself as the hired car
rocked and rattled over the cobbles of Badgerley
High Street. Badgerley, I would have you know,
is the dale's chief village. Every Saturday we sell
sheep there, and then fill up with groceries and ale.
It seemed the same as ever; even the names above the
shops were the same; though I had forgotten them
entirely, they all came back to me. And the swinging signs above the inns; and the long, lean dalesmen talking "sheep" beneath them. It was the

same, the same, the same! There was not a new
thing to be seen.

But here we are, dodging about the place as
though indeed it were a Saturday morning. And
we have still ten miles to go. But they are good
miles. After my own, I like this dale better than
anywhere in the world. We will go slowly up the
valley: we shall have to, there are so many corners.
And at every corner there is a fresh delight for you
to see.

And yet, after all, the biggest thrill comes first.
It comes from the bridge at Badgerley as you leave
the town. Just here, as you pass over the crown, if
you look very quickly straight up the river, between its trees you will see, blue and hazy—the
colour of cigarette smoke—the tops of two high,
distant hills. Those hills guard the entrance to my
valley.

You must not do as I did, though, if when you
come it is a market-day and the whole place is
thronged with lazily moving flocks of sheep and
cattle. I made my driver stop, almost blocking up
the bridge, while I looked upon those hills again.
It made me very happy to think I was as near as
that.

Then we went on, and the row of old, rook-
haunted elms which borders the road on that side

of the village shut off my view. I did not catch sight
of my hills again for quite a while, for the road
climbs up a rise just here, and all that you can see,
if you go as I did—at the proper time—are two big
banks all gay with harebells, dog-roses and wild
honeysuckle. Then you drop down again towards
the river, and the whole valley is spread out before
you. You can see the heather on the moorlands,
purply-brown; then the higher pastures, dividing
up the woodlands which come sweeping down,
some of them, right to the bottom, a bottom full of
meadows and old farms. It is like that all the way
up the dale, but the road twists and turns so much
that one never seems to be looking in the same
direction twice. Which is all to the good. There are
three little villages, wee, tiny places hiding beneath
the trees, though the first we miss entirely because
it lies across the river, a couple of hundred yards or
so up a side road. The second we go straight
through—or at least we do sometimes, for there is
a good inn there, with a village green and pretty,
flower-decked cottages—and then we cross the
river. It is near here, by the way, that they say my
river shows again, springing out from beneath a
cliff and rapidly gathering up the tribute water from
the other ghylls. The next village we also miss, just
skirting its edge, for here the road forks, dividing

into three. One branch goes into the village and dies away; the second wanders on a while towards the moor; and the third . . . the third is my little country lane, serving only scattered farms . . . and me.

We must hurry now. To be as near as this, after so long, is exquisite almost to the verge of pain. My nerves are quivering as we pass through the first trees of the wood between the cliffs. A crimson blaze of foxgloves lifts my heart bodily into my mouth . . . a little clump of silver birches, the sun full on them, in a clearing . . . young bracken . . . lichen . . . a cock pheasant flashing low across one of the rides . . . the boundary wall, all velvety with moss . . . and then the valley opening out before me, through the trees. . . .

Chapter IV

The First Pool

*

A river, to be loved, must be small, and near to its source, before it has become sophisticated. I had thought of my river as one would think of a laughing girl; a thing of youth, of joyous folly, gaiety and sunshine. I found it infantile. Could this, I wondered, on that first night as I leant over the little bridge, be the stream that I had dreamed about for half a lifetime—this little puny thing? Certainly it was late spring, and dry weather at that, but still. . . .

It would not be, at its shallowest, where even the tiniest boulders broke through the surface, more than ten yards wide; and where it ran, closely confined between the bigger rocks, or beneath the banks—its deepest—why, there I could quite easily stride across it. I could not realize that these were the deeps, the romantic, dangerous places of my childhood; the pools into which I had gazed, lying flat upon some rock, fearful lest I should slip in.

My river! My river, I realized, was still a child. It was I who had changed; I who had grown—and had forgotten. The laughter and the sunshine were the same—I realized it dimly as I stood there—but it was the happy, bubbling laughter of a child. It was a child's river. I might have known: it had been the playmate of a child; the same in growth, in happiness, in innocence. How could I have thought it would be a plaything fit for a grown man?

I walked slowly up the far bank of the stream, picking my way over the tiny sand and gravel-beds, parting the odd clumps of willow herb, striding round or over the tumbled heaps of boulders. And gradually the charm of this wee water stole over me again. I seemed to catch the echoes of the laughter I had remembered. The chuckles were infectious, like the chuckles of a baby who is amused (as no doubt it was). But there was no sound of mockery in it, not a bit; it was just in happiness, amusement. The sandpipers flitted up and down, and on every little spit of sand the wagtails pattered happily about. I felt the years slipping away. I was drawn again towards my river. More and more I remembered details of the things which had amused me in those far-off days. I forgot my idealized river—the one which had stayed with me—and I remembered the real one: how I had made dams across the tiny bays, using rocks and stones and sods, packing in the interstices with aught that I could find. How I had blocked this tiny runnel . . . and then that . . . and so made currents which would guide my boat —and by "boat" I mean any piece of stick which would float—into its particular dock. I laughed as I remembered. More and more I laughed as I felt the intervening summers fade rapidly away; and when at last I came to one wee corner, all golden sand and gravel and with half a dozen boulders placed just right, I sat me down and made another.

Yes, this was it. It was a child's river, with all the joy and laughter which goes with childhood, and with the power (rather a wonderful power, I began to think) to make even me carefree, thoughtless as a child again. That hour I spent down there was very sweet. Well, I would keep it so. I would not lose this precious asset. Whatever I did, I must not lose it.

Still, I must fish! I could not visualize my river without fish. And now I knew that the trout which I had caught in those past years, though they loomed large enough in memory, must have been, too, the captures of a child. They would not do now. The big ones I remembered? I wondered how big they really were. So when I came to a pool, a little larger than the others I had passed, I made up my mind to see. There would be a fish here: there should, by the look of it, be two or three. I rolled up my sleeve and felt under the largest rock. My finger-tips worked through the cool, soft water until they found a likely crevice; and the next moment I was touching the smooth sides of a trout. He moved slightly, over to one side, but I found him again, and very gently I brought him out. Yes, I had thought so. There he was, perhaps seven inches long, a sixth of a pound or less. What there was of him looked hard and fit; but how small, how pitifully small!

I slipped him back into the water and walked on in thoughtful mood.

But where one of the ghylls came in I got a glimpse of the river as I had, in my dreams, imagined it. Here indeed was water to delight the heart of anyone. Some cloudburst, not too recent, up in the fells and the resultant flood had brought down a mass of boulders, rock and stones. They had come tumbling down the ghyll and been thrown all the way across the main stream at right angles, piling up against the opposite bank. Ten yards thick, at least, this boulder dam would be, effectually sealing up the flow. The stream above had formed a pool; its lower half silted up, it is true, to within an inch or two of the surface with sand; but nevertheless a pool. The golden water rippled in the sunshine; a level, gently-flowing sheet; finally breaking over the dam stones in a score of little cascading runs. The stream itself, for the first half dozen yards as it entered the pool, was a sheer delight. All there was to do to make the place a really magnificent bit of fly water was to scour away that underlying sand. That would leave me a stretch of almost thirty yards in length and half as many wide.

And I did it there and then, as I will tell you.

Towards the farther side were two great boulders, standing high up out of the water, and perhaps a yard apart. So big were they that I think they must have fallen from the bank above, probably owing to the undermining of the earth beneath them. However, there they lay, the keystones of the dam. The narrow space between them was completely closed by lesser rocks; in fact all that end of the dam was dry; and of course, for some way downstream behind them were other piled-up boulders. These I started to shift. It was great fun. As I neared the two rocks, working up from below, I found the water trickling through beneath my feet.

The First Pool

More and more these trickles grew, and at last I had but half a dozen stones of any size between me and the shallowed pool above. I tugged these out, lifting and dragging them to one side, opening out completely the space between the two big rocks. The water poured down between them, at first quite clear, and then, as the level dropped and the sand began to move, in a thick and yellow turgid flood.

The pool was clear in no time—of water! Too much of the sand remained. I had got a passage, two or three yards wide, through the middle of the silt all the way down, but the sides remained still banked up with sand and stones. I went upstream, and by studied manipulation of the rocks at the head of the pool, I directed, and redirected, the main force of the water until I had all the top half clear. The middle was not too bad; but at the bottom, all the corner farthest away from the hole in the dam was piled up with sand; it seemed higher than ever, but this was due to the fallen level of the water. I hesitated to make another break in the wall. And then, as I sat resting, I noticed something which gave me an idea.

I have already explained to you how the dam was formed by a tremendous flood of storm water coming down the side-stream from Woogill. This stream still ran, of course, but now it emptied on the lower side of the dam.

It did not take me ten minutes to clear a passage on the upstream side, and I used the displaced boulders to block all other outlet. The whole force of the beck poured on to the sand in the corner and swept it across the pool and then down through the gap. I waited patiently as I could, and at last I saw the bed-rock showing through everywhere. Then, once more, I blocked the gap between the two big rocks. The water rose. It rose and rose until it overflowed in happy, delightful little runs all down the dam. As lovely a pool as ever I saw. The low sunlight danced and rippled over it. I was delighted, charmed, as happy as a king.

Well, that was that! I sat down on the bank and filled my pipe, while my eyes delighted in this thing that I had made. There was a line of alders along the farther shore, with, underneath them, a little bank of ferns and primroses, and in one place, overhanging the water, a good-sized bramble bush. The dark water underneath it looked a good place for a trout. There were many such good places when I came to look. The pool was full of them. Now if my river were all like that!

And as I got up and put on my coat, I determined that in time, in a very little time, it *should* be so.

Chapter V

Dale-Head

*

The first thing to do, of course, was to make a map. One cannot do anything without a map. On a wet day, for instance. It is a pleasant break from reading. That is why I have incorporated the map I made in this book. You will find it at the front.

I started out very thoroughly, right up on the moor, at the very beginning. So many strides to this fall, so many to that; pacing them out in the hot sunshine. But the little tumbling cascades came so frequently—every yard in some places—and the gradient fell so quickly (apart from all manner of unforeseen obstructions I did not know the marks for, and which, in any case, I should not have had room to put in) that I gave up trying. In the end, that first moorland mile of water I just put down on my chart as a little wriggly mark and started in at Outershaw, the first farmstead downstream. It is a little better there. There are occasionally—in between the madly galloping runs—what old Matt Arnison calls "dubs"—little pools a few yards long and a few feet wide.

Matt Arnison is both a shepherd and a farmer. At times the place is overrun with continuously "baaing" sheep—pasture land, meadows, the farmyard, everywhere—house as well, I dare say. At others it is infested with lean, rakish-looking cattle, which look like cannibals and can jump like stags. The latter is a trait Matt looks for: they get the pick of the grazing—other people's grazing—over half the valley. Then a week afterwards the cows are gone and the sheep are back. He must be, like all these dalesmen, a fairly shrewd judge of livestock. What he does is to buy a lot of Irish cattle; half-starved, raw-boned beasts; get them across country somehow, and up on to his moorland pastures. Some of this limestone land is good, very good, and the improvement in the poor creatures is amazing. Then, when they reach a certain pitch of rotundity, down the dale they go and Matt comes home in a state bordering upon Elysium; "market-merry", he describes it. I have met him in market myself occasionally—or supposedly in market. As a matter of fact all I have ever seen him do is to play the double-five on to a four in a tavern game of domi-

noes and actually get away with it. He has a wife:
a large, fresh-coloured body, terribly efficient at her
job (which seems to be everything) and somehow,
whatever she is doing, always spotlessly clean. She
rather frightens me, Mrs. Arnison. They have three
sons; tall, lean, raking young fellows, as big and
powerful as Matt himself; very quiet, deep-think-
ing, serious young men. They rather frighten me,
too.

But Matt! Matt is. . . .

I mentioned to him about these dams.

"Dams?" cried he, "I'll make you a dam."

We went down to find a place.

As it happened it was, to all intents and purposes,
already made. At one point in his big pasture, past
storms with their differing currents had scooped
out a long, thin, straggling depression. On the farther side the wall of rock and earth rose sheer from
the narrow stream of water flowing at its foot.
There seemed a good depth of water there even
now, but it was too fast and narrow as it was. The
river bed sloped up towards us as we stood; first a
slanting base of limestone rock, clean-swept and
shining; then stones and boulders; then sand; and
then a little lawn of grass and reedy bents and a
patch of wild rhubarb plant. And bounding this, a
wall of earth perhaps two feet high and lifting to

the flat of the pasture. From side to side the depression would be fifty feet, and it would be thirty yards long at least; a good, hefty size. We looked for a place to put the dam.

"Now look," says Matt. "If we put it there it'll but sweep round to this side, first storm that comes, and wash out another gurt hole." He looked at me with a quizzical lift of his eyebrows. "And that'll mean t'rent coming down a bit like, maybe?" That apparently suited neither of us, so downstream we went still farther. I thought the pool was going to be too big; it would have too big a drop at the bottom end for the fish to get up. I said so. "Aye, but you want to give them fish a bit of jumping exercise at times," he said. "I like to see 'em jump. It's good for 'em. They can get to t'best feeding then. Have a look at this."

We were almost at the foot of the depression, just where the belt of sand and gravel began to narrow sharply towards the water. "What's up wi' this?" he asked. "Do you want yon tree?"

The tree in question overhung the farther bank; a thick, gnarled, ugly tree, with half its branches dead and its roots twisting in and out of the rocky bank below.

"No," I said, "it would be better out of the way." I had some idea he wanted it for planks.

31

Matt turned his face towards the house. He placed his little finger knuckle in his mouth and let out a whistle which must have made everybody within a mile look round towards us.

One of his sons showed at the door of the mistal. "Bring my gurt axe," roared Matt. The boy turned inside, and in a moment or two was striding down the slope towards us. Matt took the axe from him without a word, splashed through the shallow stream, and made a studied cut in the side of the old tree. I joined him on the other bank, while the lad made his way back to the farm. In five minutes there was a deep incision all round the tree: it was supported solely by a thin pillar of hard, white, tough-looking wood in the centre. Matt looked across the stream to get his line, measured it carefully with his eye, and then made half a dozen rapid strokes with his axe. The great trunk began to heel slowly over as we stepped back; then, with a sharp crack of tearing fibres, down it pitched into the stream. There was a great splashing, a wild maelstrom of flying twigs and bits of branches, and as the hulk slowly turned over and settled down we saw what we had done. The nearer end lay well out of the water, resting on a ledge of rock and sloping gradually down to the surface of the river. In midstream the main body of the tree sprawled and

stretched, well on the bottom, reappearing on
the farther side as a tangled mass of branches and
broken wood. It ran clean across the sand and
gravel, almost up to the raised edge of the pasture
itself.

But the water still swept down the narrow channel. To me it did not seem to have risen an inch. I
said so.

Matt regarded his handiwork critically. "Now
that's just right," he said. "See them branches sticking up in t'middle yonder? Well, that's t'dam.
Thee leave it!"

I felt it was the best thing I could do. There was
one potential pool destroyed anyhow. I would do
the rest myself.

Chapter VI

Grand Tour

*

Let us get on down the river without any further interruptions. We will complete the tour. Below Outershaw the river takes a bend to the right. It is fairly fast water for two or three hundred yards, though there are quite a few "dubs" in which smaller trout could lie. They can be enlarged, I dare say, but we will leave them for the present. Let us get away from Matt Arnison just now.

The first of the bigger becks comes in at the bottom of the bend. Well, it is one of the bigger ones at times. It drains a ghyll which seems almost stood on end; a staircase of tumbled limestone rock. Just here the hills shoot up very steeply, with the result that when any water comes down at all it is a maze of waterfalls, some of them very high. After a spate, especially a summer spate, it is magnificent. The roar of it can be heard all down the valley. But

34

it has to be seen at the proper time. It is no good waiting until "tomorrow"—it will have run off then. To see that ghyll as it should be seen is a matter of Burberrys, a stout pair of boots, and a tramp through the rain. And let us hope that by the time the beck is reached, it may be fine again, with the sun splitting up the clouds, gemming the grass, and turning even the dripping trees into sparkling things of light and fire. Then indeed we shall see it at its best. The spray leaping from every fall is rainbowed; each drop a jewel in itself. And the dark, peat-coloured water transmutes the pebbles into gold. It is rich in loveliness but there are no trout.

Of course there is the making of a big pool where the ghyll joins the river. The sudden floods have scooped out quite a hole already, and the sand and boulders are spread out wide. But we will have to consider this later. It is a dangerous place to attempt a dam just yet.

There is a better place a little farther down. Here the Stonebeck comes in; and the Stonebeck is almost as big as the river itself. It comes tearing down from the fell for a mile or so, and then steadies up a little, taking tribute from the scores of little trickles and minor burns which drain the moss hags of the moor. Its bed is boulder-strewn, of course, and there are very few still places in the higher reaches.

But everywhere, to make amends, there is the happy, bubbling cadence of running water. The sides of the ghyll are steep and high and clothed with heather and tall bracken, with here and there a landslip where the limestone shale shows through, a beautiful pale lavender. Bilberry wires there are, too; sometimes in profusion. It is very fine up there on a sunny day, looking up from the bottom of the gorge, with the blue sky overhead and the great white clouds sailing grandly across.

Nobody ever goes up there, save perhaps one of the Arnisons after sheep. But it is seldom lonely. How could it be, with the curlews and the golden plover calling, and the grouse coveys crossing over —five beats and a glide—five beats and a glide— every hundred yards or so? The water in itself is a joy to hear and see. It is mostly peat, and the colour of it, in the deeper places, a rich, warm purply-brown: over the pebbled shallows it is pale and golden. There are strange lights on it sometimes, when the clouds suddenly darken and the sun is hidden. Then one sees the brooding mystery of these wild places. Old, old they seem; tremendously old; unchanged, one would imagine, from the very dawn of time. The limestone rocks seem cruel; the moss-hags a sinister menace; and the ghylls, especially the higher ghylls, take on a pall of darkness

36

which makes them look as though they might be indeed the very gates of Hell. And the silence. . . . Even the tinkling of the stream takes on a muted note. No birds call. Everywhere around is a heavy, brooding stillness, almost as though the world itself were half-afraid.

It is no good fishing at these times. I have tried; throwing off the oppression I could feel myself. But never have I caught a fish when one of these dark periods came on.

The old Romans, by the way, would know these silences. One of their roads—growing difficult to trace now, save in one or two bare places—comes straight as an arrow across the shoulder of the fell. The ford by which they used to cross the stream is still discernible, though now there are a few big boulders blocking up the way. A camp, or resting place, stood near, with, a little distance away, some building of importance. Nothing of it now is left, save the mounds over the foundations, and no one knows what it might have been.

But I will tell you what once happened to me up there.

Close by the ford, a little way above, there is a dark and cave-like hollow where the stream pitches straight down from a ledge of rock into a pool twenty or thirty feet below. Overhanging limestone rocks, all seamed and scarred, go towering up on all sides except for a narrow opening at the downstream end where the water comes out again. The pool itself, dark and mysterious, is a couple of score yards across, and deep—I don't know how deep. Mosses and ferns clothe the sides of the cliffs, reflected in the water, which, save where the fall actually enters, is very still. At no time does the sun ever reach more than a little way down the sides. The water is cold. "Icy Pool", they call it. On one side is a little beach of fine, white, quartz-like sand.

I sheltered on this little beach one evening, just on twilight. A sudden storm came sweeping down from the black recesses of the fells. One could see it approaching: a dark, menacing patch which rapidly blocked out both earth and sky. The high walls surrounding the pool would, I knew, give shelter, for the wind would carry the rain almost straight across. I ran for it.

It was warm and dry in there. I laid down my rod and composed myself to wait; watching dully the mysterious, liquid depths of the pool. It grew very dark as the heavy clouds came over; very dark and very still. All I could hear was the quiet murmur of the fall as it dropped, flume-like, into the pool. I sat there waiting for what seemed a long, long time. For a while I think I dozed.

I say I *think* I did, for. . . .

So far as I knew, I was still staring moodily at the pool, thinking of nothing in particular, more than half-asleep I dare say, though yet, I am sure, acutely conscious of all there was around me. I became aware, quite gradually aware, that the murmur of the fall appeared to be perceptibly changing—was changing even as I listened. The rise and fall of its cadences took on more definite form; seemed, in some unaccountable way, to be assuming that of actual music, though of a tone and rhythm which was strange to me. I felt a vague uneasiness stirring through my blood, as though something were all wrong somehow. This feeling passed, and I realized that other things were changing, too. The pool still lay there at my feet; but now, it seemed, much smaller. The belt of sand ran almost round it, and on the side away from me there was a level stretch of it a dozen yards or more in width and maybe twice as many long. I noticed, too, that in some way what light there was in that dark place appeared to have become intensified, almost as though the pallid brightness of the moon were reflected down on to that gleaming little space of sand. The fall was still there; though now it fell, I saw, not directly into the waters of the pool, but first upon a level ledge of rock from which it broke upwards and outwards

in a dome of glittering, diamond-studded spray.
White, gently-moving wraiths of spume filled all
that corner of the cave.

I noticed the soft lights playing upon this drifting,
fairy, mist-like water. And even as I watched I saw
the mists take shape. Etherial forms, exquisitely
beautiful and delicate—forms which glowed and
paled and faded—were even now evolving; were
dancing along the little stretch of sand across the
pool; forms lightly draped as though in some gos-
samer material which waved and glistened as they
moved. It looked like a Grecian frieze of alabaster
come to life. Six there were, six radiant young girls
dancing gloriously to the music I could still hear.
Some ceremonial dance it appeared to be; some
ritual of a beauty of which I had never dreamed.
The music softened, almost seemed to die away;
and as it did so, the dancers formed three on either
side of the dome of spray, which I saw now was
glowing as though it were the all but transparent
casket of some splendid jewel whose lambent
flames shone gently through. The six girls knelt,
as it were in worship. The pearl-like light inside
the dome grew brighter, brighter still, and I saw
the figure of a woman gradually forming through
the spray.

Then, for one brief instant, I saw her full; a

divine form, intensely white and gleaming; utterly, heartbreakingly exquisite. I could not—dared not —look upon her face, but I knew, somehow, that it was lovely beyond all imagining. One ornament alone she wore; and this—above everything, I think —I shall remember all my days. On her head there rested, gleaming pale and virginal, the horned shape of the crescent moon.

"Isis!" I breathed, and found myself upon my feet, staring at the dark waters of Icy Pool. I felt cold, benumbed, and very strange. Isis! "Isis", not "Icy" Pool. I saw now from where the possibly corrupted name might have come, and to whom the temple had been dedicated.

But then, I thought—when at last I came to think at all—surely Isis had been discredited by the Romans long before they ever conquered Britain? Diana perhaps? Could the temple have been Diana's? She, too, was goddess of the moon. Or was it possible that some sect among the invaders had still kept to the old heresies and brought them here? I do not know. All I know is that, besides being the strangest, it was the most hauntingly lovely thing that I have ever seen.

There are pools all the way down the Stonebeck, though there are too many falls, except along the last mile or so, for trout to move up freely. Where it nears the main stream, as I have said, it steadies down a bit, running through quite a delightful little valley of its own. There are a few park-like pastures along the bottom, and two good meadows. Trees there are of course, glorious trees of oak and ash and rowan, both on the river banks and scattered about the fields. On a sunny day, when the meadows are ablaze with buttercups and the larks are singing, it is very beautiful. The actual stream-bed is wide, though only a trickle of water comes down most times, and at every little bend there are wide strips of yellow, boulder-studded sand and gravel on which the sandpipers call all day. We can make dams a-plenty away up here—they are certainly needed—and a really big one at the place where stream and river join. That is if we want to. Perhaps you will be like me and, standing a little way below, looking up to where the two waters meet, decide that the place is far too lovely as it is to alter. There are other places besides this. Bear with me a little; I will show you them all.

Let us walk along the edge, beneath the shade of the bankside trees, treading easily over the short, sweet-smelling grass, down to where the next wee beck comes in—from the left this time. Here is a place, an ideal place, to fix a dam. The entering stream is not too big, barely half a mile in length in fact, and it comes in at just the proper speed, curving round obliquely so that there is no great danger of its washing out the opposite bank, even in a spate. Willow-herb grows all along one side of the main stream here; twenty or thirty yards of it. Fat caterpillars breed on these willows. Yes, we can put a good dam here.

Another trickle, smaller still, comes down a hundred yards below on the opposite side; and then another—though this is more in the nature of a large field-drain. It is almost overgrown with grass and other herbage. It lies deep-hidden under its banks, and though the water is very shallow, it is always there and flows over the most wonderful little gravel.

I have had my eye on this place for a long time. It is a great place to put down eggs or fry—but we will come to that! There are many such places. Perhaps you, like me, cannot pass even the tiniest little rill—even a road-gutter—without examining it and wondering what use it could be put to with regard to trout. At the worst we can always try it with watercress, which, they tell me, is good for both man and fish. It grows naturally; it has always done so; on the next tributary we pass. The place is almost choked with it at times. But we can thin it out. Good gravel bottom: we will make some use of this stream, too.

And now we come to the Keld Water, the third biggest of my tributary streams. Actually perhaps it is the most important of the lot, for the old pack-horse road which spans my valley follows its gradient almost to the top. This old paved track runs straight across the dale, almost at right-angles. It comes over one shoulder of the hillside to the south, zigzags down the face, joins up for a little while with the valley road which runs to Outershaw, and then branches off across the river, up the side of the Keld Water and so over the northern hills and far away. They say it goes to Scotland on the one side and to Derby on the other—or it did.

The bridge which carries it across the river is just one single fairy arch. It is barely wide enough for two persons to pass on the crown; but then that is plenty wide enough: there is never any hurry to pass there. Everyone who crosses hangs for a while over the side. They cannot help it. No doubt the old Scots packmen did the same. They came down the road from the Border Country on their way to the big cities of the West Riding and beyond, bringing with them bales of Paisley shawls and such-like luxuries. To and fro they went—for they used this road both going and returning—and everyone of them, I know, stopped to look over my bridge and watch the trout.

There is a legend, a full-blooded, melodramatic legend about an inn which once stood, a century or more ago, on the summit of the pass to the north. "Dead Man's Hill" they call it now.

At this inn, kept by a woman, a certain Maggie Thompson, and her son, these Scottish pedlars used to stay. It was one of their recognized halting places and well-known to them all; for naturally there was a great freemasonry among all these travellers; they all knew each other well. So well, indeed, that when one was missing inquiries were set on foot, casually at first and then more thoroughly. Of course there were many causes of disappearance in those days, the Press Gang, I suppose, among others. Then, too, several of them grew rich and settled either in the towns where they sold their wares or back in their own Border Country. These were known, of course, but there were several disappearances unaccounted for. Inquiries finally pointed to Dead Man's Hill—though the place was not known by that name then. Travellers going north, it turned out, had last been seen at Lothersmoor, which is a village three or four miles across the tops to the south of the valley, and those travelling south last heard of at Curryford, the final village in the next dale to the north. Between these two, almost half-way, on a bleak stretch of moorland, lay Maggie Thompson's inn. Suspicion was aroused; especially when it was also recalled that both Maggie and her relatives seemed to be more than normally well-endowed with this world's goods; Paisley shawls among them. Ponies, too, there were, scattered about the dale farms, of a breed alien to the country but similar to the ones used by the packmen.

One stout lad among these pedlars, James Angus, decided to put their theories to the test. On his next journey south—one October it was—he pulled up at the inn and asked for a night's lodging for himself, his horse and the pack-pony carrying his wares. He retired early, but did not undress and go to bed. Instead he looked round the room. His fears were confirmed by the fact of there being no lock upon the door, nor indeed any form of fastening at all. He sat upon the edge of the bed, waiting, with a cudgel, previously concealed beneath his coat, ready to his hand. In spite of himself, he had almost dozed off to sleep when he heard muttered voices below. And then a creak upon the stairs. In the almost darkness he saw the door slowly open. James did not wait. He cracked the intruder, Maggie Thompson's son, over the head, and with his next blow sent the knife which the woman was holding spinning on to the floor. Then out of the window on to his horse and away for assistance.

He got it, too. He came back with half Lothersmoor. Maggie and her son were arrested and investigations set afoot. Three bodies were actually found, buried under the trees of a little copse which is still standing—though the trees will have been replaced by others now—and in time both Maggie and her son were hanged. There are variations of the legend: some say the trunks were buried on one side of the hill and the heads on the other, I suppose to prevent identification. However this may be, the name of the hill was changed. It is now known everywhere as "Dead Man's Hill".

The Keld Water is very fast. It comes pounding down from the moor in a thousand little falls and runs. It is full of tiny trout, but a difficult place for us to improve in the normal way. Dams, sufficient to make pools of any size, would have to be, of necessity, too high at the bottom for fish to get up. But there are many little holes where there is just room enough to drop an odd fly and it is really a very delightful, invigorating stretch of water. Those fish run small, though. We must alter that.

The last three or four furlongs, where it runs through the meadows, are good. That length is almost as good as the river. I have it all planned out and will tell you about it later. I bear it in mind as a good place to maroon a guest who likes—or, more important, whom I like—to be alone. I will make it a day's job for him, that odd half mile or so of water.

Where the beck joins the river there is a broad stretch of shallow. I should say that just there it is the widest part in the whole valley. Big boulders stand up everywhere, and the whole bed of the stream is littered with smaller stones. Very fast water, no holes of any size, and most unprofitable to fish. And then, to make a bad length worse, some little way below there is a fall of perhaps eight or ten feet over a limestone ledge into a shallow pool below.

The fall itself, of course, is picturesque enough in its own way. It looks well in times of spate, with the water shooting over in a broken sheet of brown and white and the dark rocks jutting through. It has certainly an attraction then, too good to lose. But in dry spells it is not so good. At those times there are merely bare, grey slabs of limestone rock to look at, with all the fall there is a narrow foot-wide column dropping down into the pool below. I will tell you later how I actually increased its flood-time appeal and also made it possible for fish to move easily up or down, and how I, at the same time, turned a stony, barren stretch into one of the best bits on the river.

Below the fall comes in Burngill. Burngill is a good stream with a lovely gravelled bottom and banks which are deeply undercut. It is not wise to walk too near the edge, for often the whole turf caves in and one goes wet-shod for a while. It is a very popular spawning stream, and Burngill I think we had better leave as it is.

Let us get on.

Any number of little trickles are coming in now, not big enough to harbour fish, but very good for planting out with cress and marigolds and such; breeding grounds for trout food if not for trout. One's optimism grows as the lower reaches come into view. We are in among the meadows now, and every runlet must bring down a deal of food. All of them have rich, luxuriant banks, overhung with ferns and meadowsweet and water-plants— great places for insect life. Two more little becks, tumbling down from narrow ghylls, cut into the mountain side, and then Woogill.

Woogill is the biggest of all the burns which feed the river. I have already told you how I turned Woogill into the main stream at a different angle and so made my first big pool. Like the others it is boulder-strewn and very fast, but there are runs and pools already there which, with a very little manipulation, can be made into delightful water. Trees there are along its banks—not too many of them—and a row of elms which are one of the heirlooms of the valley. A couple of farms lie on the banks, too. One belongs to old John Lister, whose family has been here five or six hundred years and who tells the biggest lies about St. Leger "certainties" of any man I know. The other one is rented to Jim McLeod, a newcomer to this farm and a son of old Will McLeod who won prizes at sheepdog trials in all three Kingdoms. He broke in his puppies teaching them to round up and "mind" little flocks of ducks. I spent many hours with old Will when I was a lad. He taught me a lot. Under his tuition I got a couple of fox terriers to do what most of the expensively trained gundogs I used to see could not.

But that is by the way. If I tell you about old McLeod I am taking you away from the river up on to the moors, for that is where he mainly spent his time; counting up and caring for his sheep presumably, but really, I think, because the wildness of those higher levels reminded him of Skye.

Woogill were we at? We will come back again to Woogill later. There is a lot of work to be done there.

Three or four more little tributaries, and then Morraside Beck; rougher, wilder than the others. It drains a cleft which is almost wholly bare, grey limestone. High cliffs go towering up from its narrow gorge in the hills. Pigeons, odd kestrels, starlings, all manner of birds breed on its sides. Its bed is apparently composed of flat and level rectangular slates; no stones hardly at all—just these polished flats of limestone rock. It is up Morraside Ghyll where the subterranean caverns are. One first enters them through a small, round tunnel. In places along its hundred yards or so of length it is head-high; at others barely a couple of feet or so; and everywhere is very wet, with limey water oozing from the roof and sides, and brittle stalactites of an inch or two in length hanging from every little ledge. As I say, a hundred yards inside, the tunnel ends. It gives place to a great and roomy cavern where, almost instinctively, one speaks softly for fear the roof will fall. And from this central place, cavern after cavern opens out, some on one level, some on others; some reached by further tunnels, others by gaunt archways reminiscent of those of a cathedral. Everywhere there is the immediate or distant sound of falling water, and at one place the floor of the cave abruptly ends in a ledge of rock and in front there is nothing but a great yawning blackness like the very Pit. A stone thrown over goes down and down and then down. How far I do not know, nobody knows. One cannot hear a sound once the stone has left one's hand; not even the faintest tinkle. A nasty, dark place that!

Stalactites there are, of course, in numbers; most of them fairly big, too, inside here; but they have nothing of the fairy shapes some others have that I have seen elsewhere.

I would not like to get lost in these gloomy places. I believe the whole hillside must be hollow. Let us get out.

Below Morraside, maybe a couple of hundred yards away, another stream comes in: Foggyshaw. Up in our country a "shaw" is any fairly open bit of land, but whether the "foggy" refers to climatic conditions hereabouts in some distant age—for the name is very old—or whether it has to do with "fog", the aftergrowth of meadow-grass, I do not know. It might be either, for the beck takes its rise high up on the mountain tops, where there is often misty cloud, and also runs through half a dozen of the lushest meadows that we have. It is a pretty stream; in its lower levels it might have been lifted whole from some much softer land than ours. It is wider than most of the others, and its banks more luxuriant. Primroses, violets, a host of flowers enrich its sides; bushes of dog-rose and briar keep guard over some of the best holes in its more trouty lengths, making the casting of even one odd fly a matter of nicety and judgment. The cheery dippers haunt its mossy boulders, building year after year in the angle of the bridge which spans it a hundred yards from its junction with the river. I mention dippers especially, for I love them, but there are many other birds who also have made Foggyshaw their own: wrens and robins, all three sorts of wagtails, sandpipers, blackbirds and thrushes, odd redstarts, flycatchers—oh, a host of birds. And I, too, have made Foggyshaw my own, for Foggyshaw is where I live. My garden runs down to the edge of the burn. A low, grey-lichened wall, with saxifrage and such-like plants growing on it, is all there is between my grass and the clear, brown laughing water. It is a pleasant place to sit in the cool of a June night, when the scent of hay is everywhere, and the whaups are calling from the moorlands above. One leaves it with regret as one sees the luminous belt of green where the sun has set go creeping eastwards behind the hill and show again on the other side. The summer nights are very short away up here. Too soon it is the coming of another day.

Once more have I led you astray. But the walk

from here, only a few hundred yards or so, back to the river is very dear to me. And if we look over the banks we shall certainly see some trout. Good water this will prove in time; a very little time now; for I intend to tell you in the very next chapter, how I built all my dams and started in to make my river what it is. But first we must finish our tour. It is not far now.

Where Foggyshaw comes in—Foggyshaw Foot —there is a little pool already, and then the river goes once more galloping away. We shall enlarge it later, making it—as it should be, standing so near my house—one of the best bits on the river. A sister beck comes in on the opposite side, a score yards lower down. Our pool will embody the outlets of them both. And then, a couple of furlongs lower still, my river ends. The scattered birches grow more frequent. They are the outposts of my guardian wood, lying there before us now we have turned the last sharp corner. The two great cliffs are there, with their craggy summits clear-cut against the sky; and between their feet the whole depth of the wood, with just a narrow ride cut through and along which there runs a thin white ribbon of road which leads, I will tell you now, in case you want to go, back to the open country and the towns and cities and all the other haunts of men.

Grand Tour

But I will show you Gurston Pot first. It is just here: a grim, tunnel-like hole cut into the side of one of the cliffs, and through which the water roars and tumbles in wild disarray. There is a fall not far inside the entrance, but it is not very deep—just sufficient to fill the cavern with a riot of noise and to hide the actual way the river turns. One sees the whitened water go shooting out towards this ledge and then—just disappear. Beyond is darkness—the unknown. For me it is the end of all things: I lose my river there.

Chapter VII

Boulder Dams

*

I started in to make my dams within a week or so of my arrival. There were many things to do, of course, round about the house and garden, and a great many people to attend to on various matters. But to me—though nobody else seemed to realize it—there was nothing just so urgent as these dams. I held quite important interviews in my shirt-sleeves down at the water-side, speaking to black-coated persons between gasps as I tugged and heaved at boulders and rolled them into place. Some glared bleakly at me, doubtless interpreting the various remarks I addressed to recalcitrant stones as pointing to themselves: others merely regarded me with a pitying sort of smile and registered a mental note to charge me double. I did not care what they did so long as they went away quickly. After my experience with Matt Arnison I intended to do things myself.

But, apart from these parasites, it was delightful down there. That first week of June was one succession of blazing days. The river, as I have mentioned, was ridiculously low to begin with, and it went on shrinking every day. I feared that, if I did not hurry, it would go altogether. I made half a dozen boulder dams, one each day, at what I thought were suitable places. First I located a stretch where there would be three or four good, big boulders fairly close together and going, more or less, across the stream. To these I would roll any other big ones I could find lying about. Of course, as is the way of things, the stones I wanted most were always deeply embedded in the stream itself, and these I had to heave out by means of a pick and crowbar. Then I would trundle them down, one by one, into what I thought would be the best places for them. It was hard work, and I soon found out that it was sound policy to leave the downstream rocks alone, however attractive they might look. They seemed to take ten times the handling and never somehow fitted in. And naturally I had to lever these uphill: the others moved, at least a little, on the slope, and where, as occasionally happened, I dug one up out of the water and rolled it down actually along the stream bed, it moved easily.

The bigger boulders once in position, I packed

up the interstices with smaller ones, and then with just ordinary little bits of rock and stones. Odd turfs and lumps of moss which came handy I used as well, filling in all the gaps which I could find, until the trickles actually percolating through the dam were negligible. I worked like a slave at some of those dams. True, only a cupful of water was coming down now, but I could tell by the size of the gravel-beds and the dimensions of some of the boulders themselves what a real spate would be like and the damage it could do. I did not intend my dams to be washed away and the results of my toil squandered over the next half mile or so down-stream. I made those dams strong; some of them would be three yards thick. One or two layers deep only; I realized it would be futile to attempt to build upwards, even had I wanted to. But as it was, my dams would raise the water—when there was any!—a good three feet, and that was enough. And they were strong. I rejoiced in the thought of how strong they were.

Taking a rough level, I estimated that three of my pools would each be a good thirty yards long. The others would be smaller, but as these last three happened to lie fairly close together I did not mind that; in fact I liked it better. One could—or would be able to—fish up one pool to the very top and then, in a couple of strides or so, be fishing the one above. They came down, one behind the other, in terraced steps. Not regular steps, of course: I broke up most carefully all suggestions of hard or uncouth lines. Always I kept before my eyes the thought that I must not change in the slightest the character of my stream. I loved it as it was too well for that.

I finished the last of these late one afternoon, and to fill in the odd half hour I had to spare, I decided to walk upstream a little way and find exactly where to start another series. Even as I put on my coat I could see the dam I had just completed filling in. It was surprising, once I had closed up the outlets fairly well, how rapidly the water spread over the level bits in the centre and then gradually crept up the sides. By the time I left it, the bottom was already covered halfway across the lower part of the pool.

I was away a little longer than I expected. As I drew level with young Jim McLeod's farm, perhaps five hundred yards above the topmost of my dams, I could hear an endless baa-baa-baaing coming down from the paddock above his house. A moving cloud of disconsolate grey sheep wandered here and there about the adjoining pasture; and, on the other side of a little stream which came tumbling down from the moorlands above, I could make out the pens where another flock was tightly herded. Sheep-washing, obviously. I wandered up to see how they were getting on.

I was interested immediately. They had dammed the little beck across a narrow part where it ran through a fairly deeply cut channel between two rocks; and their method of damming was a quicker one than mine. Four flat planks had been wedged upright, one on top of the other, against the rocks; and above this impromptu dam the water had welled up until a pool had formed perhaps three or four feet deep and a dozen or so yards long. It was extremely efficient, but very ugly. After the first glance I dropped the incipient idea of board dams. I was not going to spoil the beauty of my river with a series of atrocities like that. But I had a notion, all the same, that the idea might come in useful. Worked in conjunction with my more natural-looking boulder dams, the things would possibly help me out at some unchancy, difficult place or other. I would remember.

Young Jim and his shepherd were waist-deep in the water, clad in rubber thigh-boots—though why I do not know; they shipped a gallon or two every time a fresh sheep came down—and another lad moved about among the animals in the pen, catch-

ing hold of one as required and half pushing, half
carrying the struggling, kicking beast down the
gangway to the water. It went in with a resounding
splash, and as it came to the top again, was in-
continently grabbed by one of the two men and
given a thoroughly good dousing. Then, in chas-
tened mood, it was allowed to struggle out on the
opposite side and join the others wandering for-
lornly about the pasture.

I watched until they had finished and young Jim
clambered out beside me. He gave a nod to the man
who had been in the pool with him and the latter
ripped out the four planks one by one and threw
them on to the bank. The pool was emptied in a
couple of minutes.

"That's the sort of dam you want to build,"
smiled Jim, with a twinkle in his eye. "No chance
of *that* silting up!"

Silt! I had forgotten about silt! And with the
memory of my Woogill dam—the one I had made
first of all and had cleared by means of turning in a
side-stream—still only a week or two old. Of
course my dams would silt up! The very first
freshet which came down would fill them to the
brim with sand and gravel and all I would have
done would be to have raised the bed of the
stream three or four feet higher than it was before.

I felt my blood go thin at the thought of it.

I toyed with the idea of the rehabilitated board dams all the way back to the main stream. They were good: no doubt about that. All I actually need do was to fix up two or three good strong planks across and I would have my dam. Then, when the floods came, bringing down their loads of sand and gravel—which, of course, would be deposited against the boards; backing upstream, it may be, until the whole bed of the pool had been filled up level with the top of the planks—all I had to do was to lift out the boards and let the water sweep the deposit away downstream. Then, when the place was clear again, I would put my dam back once more and presto! I had my pool, as fresh and clean as ever, in half an hour.

Yes, board dams were good; no doubt about that.

But they were very ugly. When I reached the river again and saw the rippling water playing in and out among the moss-covered stones; and the harebells on the banks; and the pleasant sun-warmed beaches of sand and gravel—when I saw the natural loveliness of it all and thought how I should spoil it —once more I put the idea of board dams completely out of mind. No, no, no. They could never be! All the beauty and the laughter and the happiness I loved so well would be destroyed. Silt or no silt, I must find some other way.

I made out the glint of level water a hundred yards before I reached my dam. It was full already, even overflowing. Down I hurried, swinging out wide in a detour as I drew nearer so that I should first approach it from below. I wished to see exactly how my stone dams compared with young Mc-Leod's—in looks, of course; I had immediately surrendered on the score of their efficiency. Ah, no; there was no comparison! Here was my dam; a broken line of boulders of every shape and size and colour, just flung as it were haphazardly across the stream, and with the water breaking over in the most delightful little falls and trickles, some large, some small, infinitely varied; and all of them making little streamy runs as they fell into the shallow water at the head of the next pool below. For here, you may remember, I had made three dams close together and the water held up by each reached to the foot of the one above. They came down in three deeply-terraced steps: three pools of exquisite charm as they lay there beneath the trees, with the low sunlight just glinting on them here and there through the branches.

I drew level with the dam wall itself, moving up from below, and as I reached it a dark shadow

streaked across to the shelter of a stone on the far
side. My heart jumped. So soon? The place was
barely an hour old, and here already there was a
fish. And it looked a good one, too! I was across
those boulders in a flash, my coat off, and my fingers
probing carefully among the crevices of the rock
under which he had gone. I had him out in no time,
handling him carefully; and then, after one look,
back I slipped him into the water again. My heart
exulted; though surprise, I think, was uppermost in
my mind. Where had he come from: how had he
found my dam in this short time? And his size? It
was his size which startled me the most of all. For
that fish I had just handled would weigh a full
three-quarters of a pound!

I was very late that evening getting home. No
fish were showing in the centre pool of the three,
for I had approached that unheedingly when I came
to view my upper dam, and had doubtless scared any
trout there might have been. But the lowest one I
stalked from well below, crawling on hands and
knees and taking shelter from every piece of cover I
could find. At first I could see nothing, and then, as
my eyes slowly worked upstream, I made out the
forms of not one, but three good fish laid almost in
a row. They were sheltering behind a big, upstanding rock which heaved its shoulder high above the

surface. Three good fish, the smallest of them a quarter of a pound at least.

And then, a few yards higher up, I saw three more!

I found fish in all six of my pools. I walked on air.

Chapter VIII

Ridsdale

*

There have been no conversations in this book so far—or very few—and, as Alice said, "what is the use of a book without conversations?"

But though I have not mentioned them particularly, it is not because there were none. There were quite a number. And almost every one of them annoyed me, especially that one of Jim McLeod's which mentioned silt. Once I had recovered from my elation at finding that, after all, there actually were good fish in my stream, and the pardonable pride I felt in having made my dams so attractive to them, there returned to me, with redoubled irritation now, this disturbing question of silt. I knew full well how true it was. Now I came to think of it, every little pool that I had ever seen seemed to have had a shallow, shelving bank of sand at its downstream end. I shuddered to think what my

66

bigger ones would be like. It looked as though my efforts would indeed only have made matters worse, for the sand and gravel which would be deposited would cover up all the stream-bed boulders and do away with what few natural shelter-places there already were.

Nor had I long to wait to prove it. That very night a belt of cloud came rolling up, full-sailed, from the south-west. I watched it coming; first a tiny pyramid of black poking up over the horizon and then, as it came nearer, a vast bulk rearing up into the sky. The hills under it turned indigo, then black, then faded out altogether. The clouds came on, clear-cut, dark against the pale blue of the sky. In half an hour it was raining hard, and in another it was a deluge. The little stream in front of my house—Foggyshaw—swelled and roared until it could be heard above all other sounds. Already the water was coming down thick and dark, only the whitened wave caps showing in the gloom. I could see it rising minute by minute, climbing higher up the wall at the foot of the garden, spreading wider over the sloping flats of the other bank.

It went on for hours. It was raining as hard as ever when I went to bed. "Well, that settles it," thought I, as I turned in. "I shall know all about silting-up in the morning."

But it was still raining when I awoke. I hung about a long time indoors, but my anxiety was too great. I slipped on wet-weather kit and splashed my way down through the soaking pastures to the river; to the first pool I had made.

I could distinguish neither boulders nor silt when I finally got there, nor indeed any sign of my dam at all. A wavering bulge showed at odd times on the surface of the water—perhaps that was it! All there was to see was a thick, brown torrent tearing away, bank-high, downstream; bringing with it all manner of obscene rubbish; bits of railing; tree-branches; an old newspaper; two or three half-empty but still corked bottles; all manner of things.

I went back home.

Well, there was nothing I could do there either; nothing, that is, which would help my dams. I decided to run down to Badgerley, where I knew some people, in search of sympathy.

I did not get so far. As I believe I have told you before, halfway down the dale, some way below where my river comes out again on the surface, there is a really delightful little village—shall we call it Raygill?—where there is an inn. I had discovered, a mile or two back, that I had come out without tobacco and I swung in across the green and pulled up at the inn door. Inside I could see the landlord talking to another man, a stranger, across the bar; a man with half a dozen trout flies stuck in his hat.

Soon it was I who was doing the talking. I liked this fellow. He was older than I was by a good bit, but the wrinkles about his eyes, in fact everything about him appealed to me. Ridsdale, they called him, and he had come up for a few days' fishing. He too passed adequate remarks about the quantity and the quality of the water coming down.

Excellent ale they keep at that inn! From ale we went to lunch, and from lunch to talk about my dams. We talked all afternoon. Silt—of course my dams would silt up! he said. But even then, I had done good; my labour would not have been wholly in vain. Ridsdale told me how, at the least, my dams, even though silted up, would keep submerged—if only under the shallowest water—a good bit of gravel-bed which was not covered before. By this I had increased, by just so much, the breeding-ground of the aquatic flies upon which to a great extent my fish depended for their food. Good! I felt brighter already. I liked Ridsdale more and more. I passed an order into the bar.

Still: I wanted pools to fish in, not to breed flies in!

I said so.

Board dams again! A tentative suggestion; but I explained to Ridsdale how I felt about board dams. My point was appreciated—at which I do not wonder, for, though the only drawing material he ever seemed to carry was a corkscrew, I found out that, among other things, he was an A.R.A.

We talked loftily a while on Art, and then, reverting to my dams, this wonderful man suggested that I use wire-netting!

I began to think that the ale was even better than I thought—either that, or he had suddenly gone mad.

I coughed discreetly. "Wire-netting, did you say?"

"Yes, wire-netting. One inch mesh would be the best for your water, I should imagine." He rolled his eyes upwards as it were in thought. "Yes, one inch mesh, about five feet wide."

He *had* gone mad! No ale could make a man talk like that. I gazed at him bleakly.

"And how do you use this—er—wire-netting?" I asked.

"Oh, just stretch it across from side to side; stake it in the middle, or where you think fit, for extra support, and lay about two-thirds of it flat on the river bed, upstream side of the stakes. Chuck a few boulders and some gravel on this flat bit to hold it down, and fasten the upright netting to the stakes. You'll have to make it very strong. You see the idea?"

"No," I said, suddenly bold.

He scowled at me over the top of his spectacles.

I crossed my fingers. "It *was* wire-netting you said?" I quavered, hoping against hope.

"Of course I said wire-netting. What did you think I said?"

I thought it was time to sue for peace. Humour them—that was the way to treat these fellows, I remembered. "Yes," I agreed, brightly, waiving his question aside; "yes, that would get over the difficulty. They would not be half so conspicuous as board dams."

"Oh, I wouldn't say that exactly," he demurred. "They'll fit in better perhaps with the surroundings; but when you get a two or three feet thick layer of leaves and grasses and other rubbish banked up against your wire, they'll be conspicuous enough."

It flashed upon me then. Of course! Every twig or wisp of hay or anything which came down would be caught on the upright netting and stay there. In time they would effectually seal the flow. Gravel and sand would cover the buried flat portion of the wire and hold it firm to the bottom. The stakes—already I had in mind designs for camouflaging those stakes—would hold the upright portion fast, along with wing-stays fastened to the bank. I saw it all.

"You are right," I exclaimed, doubly enthusiastic in my relief to find he was not mad and at his idea. "I believe you've solved my difficulty."

He smiled knowingly. "Wait and see," he remarked. "You don't know what these dale floods can do. I remember once. . . ."

But I am not going to tell you what he remembered. In fact I have forgotten myself. But when at last I did get down to Badgerley I bought a great deal of wire-netting and ordered more.

The idea of these wire dams appealed to me. They were easy to make; were cheap; and from what Ridsdale had said they would last for years. Already I had thought of a score of places where I could put them; where they would fit in with the surroundings and look almost accidental. I intended to experiment a little with those weirs. I was not going to have them just stretched straight across. I meant to break up their hard lines and twist them in and out a little, winding them about between the boulders in midstream and the banks—work them, in fact, much as I had done my other dams.

The rain had stopped by the time I reached home, and already, as is usual on these moorland streams, the storm water had run off a great deal. The beck in front of the house had dropped a couple of feet or more and was no longer muddy; merely a full, rich, porter-coloured flow through which, in the shallower places, I could see the bottom. The bank-side weeds and grasses over which it had spread were laid out almost flat, their heads pointing downstream, and every here and there were little pools which had not yet drained away.

The river itself, I knew, would be still too full for me to make out how my dams had stood. In fact, judging by the glimpses I had of it as I came up the dale, I had very little hope of being able to see any-thing for another twenty-four hours at least. But I did not worry so much now. Ridsdale's talk had altered all that. I went back indoors and drew im-aginary plans of how I would dodge those strips of wire-netting across my stream. I made a memo to see George—George was the man who pottered about my garden and gave me bills to pay for plants and things he said "we" needed—about some stakes. These stakes I meant should be natural ones; branches of trees carefully cut and trimmed so that, in addition to being strong enough, they should look as though they were just old roots and things which had been lodged there naturally. I was hav-ing no "four-by-threes" and so forth stuck up at regular intervals across my river and then, when my friends came up, have them asking me if I were keeping ducks.

I made a memo of it, as I say. As though I should forget! I knew, even as I wrote it, that I should be after George before I had had my breakfast.

And so I was. I found him, with a couple of hours work already behind him, on hands and knees among the roses. He straightened up as he saw me approach and smiled. There is something almost saintly about these old men who live in gardens. It is as though they themselves had absorbed something of the peace and fragrance of the trees and flowers they work among. I was a thousand generations nearer the primeval than George. For him the cultured beauty of a garden: for me—ah, for me the hills and the streams, the woods and the fields, the heather and the pines and the dancing waters. I was never happy unless I were among all these. Always the whaups were calling me to the wilder places. Always. Always. Always.

I explained to George exactly what I wanted; and he told me of an elm which had fallen in the storm of the night before. How he had known of it I do not know, for it was a couple of miles up the valley. I could almost imagine it was telepathy; for

George seemed somehow to be in intimate touch with everything which grew. I suppose that actually one of the keepers must have told him. But anyhow, there were my stakes, in embryo as it were.

And now to have a look at my boulder dams. I made my way down through the watery sunshine to the river. So far as I could see it had not altered much. There were the sandy gravel-beds, still much the same as they had been before, still showing bright and golden where the sunlight fell upon them through the trees. More water was in the stream; but not so much as I had expected. The moss-covered rocks and boulders still split up the currents into dancing rills which laughed and bubbled noisily over the shallows. I could see but very little change at all.

Until I reached the first of my dams!

My heart sank as I caught sight of it. Water there was, certainly, and flowing over the full width of it. But water of a depth of three or four inches only. The whole of the upstream bed of the river was coated with a thick layer of sand and gravel. It looked as smooth and level as a billiard table. For twenty yards back, almost the full length of the pool, it had silted up. Only at the top was there any sign of my handiwork at all, and here of course the water was naturally shallow to begin with. I had raised the bed of the stream a couple of feet or so and that was all.

Well, that was one day's toil gone for nothing, anyhow! And when I dragged myself up as far as the next two I found that a further forty-eight hours work had gone too. They were just the same as the others: silt up to the very head of the pool. I wasted no more time there. I would look at the whole six and get quite properly depressed while I was at it.

The next three, you may remember, I had made close together; three pools one below the other, each about twenty yards long, dropping down in a series of flat terraces and only separated, one from another, by the boulder dams I had thrown across the full width of the river.

I came up to the lowest from below. Silt again; worse, it appeared, than any of the ones downstream. But a few yards higher up my heart gave a sudden leap. Instead of shallowing, as it should have done, the water deepened! It deepened until under the higher dam wall itself the pool would be six or eight feet deep! At least! I flew up to the pool above. It was the same. The one above that, the topmost of the series, I did not bother about, for I knew that it would be the same as those others I had seen at first. But these two! They were good. I saw what had happened plainly. The force of the water coming over the fall had scooped out a hole immediately underneath it and gone on scooping and scooping and scooping. The gravel it had scoured out had certainly been deposited against the next obstruction downstream, namely the dam above the pool below, but what did that matter? The average depth of water was still there. All the flood had done was to deepen the water at the top end instead of, as I myself had done, at the bottom. These two pools were still as big and as wide, and I should say, on the average, deeper than I had made them. Splendid!

And the boulder dams themselves looked fine; fine and bold and strong. They looked as though they had been there for ever.

In series—in terraces—half a dozen or more at a time—that was how I should have to build my dams in future.

And that is how I did eventually build them. The top pool of the stairway—if one can describe it so—was always wasted. The first flood filled it; backing it up with silt and gravel, and sometimes heavier stuff, for a dozen yards or more. But the pools below were *good*. In every case they were deep immediately beneath the fall and for some way downstream, shelving gradually towards the tail and leaving maybe six inches—perhaps a foot in places —of water only. Then the stream would plunge over the dam wall and scoop out another hole. They were lovely pools. I had been careful to leave no suggestion of straight lines anywhere; fixing the stones in a haphazard-looking row so as to break up every suspicion of artificiality. They blended well with the rock and boulders now exposed on the stream-bed for the first time. There were countless little runs and eddies twisting about these boulders; ample shelter for all the trout there were.

Chapter IX

Marigolds and Watercress

*

And these fish of mine—how had *they* gone on? There had been one in the topmost pool; he would have gone—or else was buried a foot deep under the silt. But the half dozen in the lowest? I wondered how they had weathered the flood.

I would go away for an hour and then come back to see.

The stalk I put in up towards that lowest pool would have done credit to a Pawnee Indian. A hundred yards away I began to crouch, and the last thirty I crawled on hands and knees. I took shelter behind every bush; behind every blade of grass almost; and I came out, flat on my stomach and hitching myself forward by my elbows, just halfway up the pool. I lay, well-hidden, behind a clump of meadow-sweet, which I gently parted so that I could see. The light was exactly right. It shone down in great, wide patches through the trees, illuminating

79

every pebble on the river's bed. The golden water, run off now to the colour of lager beer, was clear and transparent; a perfect fly-water. I looked about for my fish.

The first sign of them I caught was a perfect ring appearing on the surface some few yards below me. And then another—and another. Why, there was a rise on! In a minute the whole surface of the pool was rippled by these entrancing rings. Up towards the head, where the tiny runs came down from the pool above, there seemed to be a dozen trout at least, all keenly on the feed. Just opposite to where I lay things seemed fairly quiet. Soon, however, I saw a good half-pounder come cruising into view and, following him, a couple more almost as big. Yet when I looked, the number of those rings, both above and below me, did not seem to have diminished. Why, thought I, there must be a score of fish in the pool!

And so there was. I crawled up and down the edge for half an hour and I saw them all. Oh, this was excellent! Why, if I wanted, I could fish there now. Whether it was the deeper water, or the covering over of the gravel-beds, or what, I neither knew nor cared. Sufficient for me, at the moment, was the fact that the trout were there. I hated leaving that pool; but my exhilaration would not let me stay. I wished to see what there was in the middle pool of the three.

And there again, when I raised myself up to look, I saw those delightful rings. All the way up they seemed to be; and there was no doubt about it, the best places—just on the edges of the runs and among the rippled water at the tail of the stream— had been taken permanently. Rise after rise came up at the same spot; time after time. I could have covered each of those trout's wanderings with a dinner-plate.

Where the fish had come from I do not know. I seldom saw any in the little runs and holes of the stream itself as I moved up and down. But obviously there were plenty of trout hidden away somewhere. All they wanted were pools to congregate in. Pools and pools and pools—in terraces. I had found the secret of boulder dams. They had to be built in terraces, one below the other, touching. The top dam would make no permanent pool above it; but it would below; and that was all I wanted. What cared I whether the pool be deepest at the head or the tail? It mattered not to me. I could break up the rather monotonous-looking beds of silt at the lower ends, too. I did it there and then. I fetched my pick and crowbar from the tree root where I had placed them and levered half a dozen big, rough half-ton boulders into the stream at different places where I thought it needed them. They broke up the surface admirably; splitting up the flat bed of silted gravel in quite attractive fashion. I stepped back in the end and looked over those two pools in sheer delight.

Pools—pools—more and more pools! For the next fortnight I did nothing but make pools. Hay-time had started in the valley and there were no lads available to give me a hand. George was busy in the garden. I had to do the work myself; hard, navvying work. But did I care? Not I. I could hardly tear myself away. The sound of the river; the bubbling, laughing cadences of every yard of it; the happy chirruping of the bankside birds; the scent of hay; the endless sunshine; the work itself—and the promise it held out—I was very happy down there.

I made all my boulder dams in series. Sometimes I would find a place where I could throw half a dozen across, each twenty or thirty yards below the one above. I varied the lines of them: some I made fairly straight; others I wove in and out among the rocks and boulders already there. As I say, I broke up the lines as much as possible, both in height and width. Those rough stone dams fitted in remarkably with their surroundings by the time that I had done with them.

It was only where the river fell rather rapidly

that I could make these terraced pools. The longer runs, where the water flowed more or less evenly over flat stretches of rock and shale, I left for my wire-netting experiments. They would come later. I should want help with those. Even a couple of yards of wire-netting is an unchancy, fiendish thing to handle by oneself: I dared not think what I should be like trying to manipulate a bit the length of a cricket pitch on uneven ground, and with part of it under water at that. Those wire weirs would simply *have* to wait.

But I found that there was plenty that I could do. My dams all filled up beautifully and kept their shape. I realized that the first flood down would alter them; but so long as they were in steps, or terraces, I knew they would be just as good. I did not worry about them further. And they all held trout. It was a never-failing miracle to me where these fish came from. I would finish making a pool, and I would have guaranteed that there was not a trout in it, anywhere. Then I would go away for an hour, and when I came back there would be two or three, perhaps more. Whether they came up or down I never knew. But they got there, big and little ones too.

The sight of these smaller fish set me off wondering how I could increase their size. I had seen plenty

—well, a good number anyway—of quarter-pound fish; some few towards the half-pound; and one at least which weighed a full three-quarters. Why should I not have pounders, too? It was mainly a question of food; that I already knew; and although, as my friend at the inn had told me, my increased water surface would improve the supplies of nymphs and other insects, that was not enough. It was not going to be anyhow.

I set about learning how to feed fish.

Now I had noticed, at the foot of Foggyshaw, how there were always two or three trout in position not far from the outflow, though not quite in it. It was rather a good natural pool to begin with and, at first, I put it down to that. It was when I got home one afternoon that the real reason dawned upon me. I found George washing a huge, fresh bunch of watercress which he had brought up to the house. The whole bottom of the white enamelled bowl he was using was covered with tiny fresh-water shrimps; little wriggly things which twisted and turned all ways in the water or settled down upon the washed-out grains of sand, and among these grains of sand were a dozen or more fresh-water snails as well. Fish-food!

"Where did this come from, George?" I asked.

"Down Foggyshaw bottom. There's a bed there,

sir, just lying off the stream. You'll have seen it, likely, many a time. Rare good watercress it is too."

Foggyshaw bottom. I knew it! That was why those fish were always hanging about that pool. I took George by the shoulder. "Leave that, George, and come with me. I want to see that bed."

He dropped the watercress back into the bowl, wiped his hands on the seat of his trousers, and shambled along beside me almost to the foot of the beck. In a little marshy hollow, standing back a few yards from the stream and fed by a dozen seeping places in a tiny limestone bluff which overhung it, lay a bed of watercress twenty or thirty yards across. Little runlets where the water trickled gently over the gravel showed here and there, and there was one white patch where George's bunch had obviously been cut away. The marsh drained out into the main stream by means of half a dozen gently flowing little trickles; not big enough for a trout to get up, but strong enough to wash down any shrimps there might be lying loose. I parted the deep green leaves of one thick growth of cress, and there, on the bottom or stuck to the whitish stems of the plant, were not just odd ones or twos, but hundreds of the little clear-bodied shrimps. At one side, near the bluff, were half a dozen rocks and what had once been a thorn bush. The green algal growths on these, when I looked at them, seemed to be alive with snails and spawn.

"George," I cried, "I want watercress planted everywhere it will grow; in all the little runnels; all the odd corners; all the way up the river."

"Aye, aye, sir. Is it these shrimps or the snails you've got your eye on?"

"Both, George, both. There's enough food there to feed. . . ."

"That may be, sir; but tha' knaws" (George always slipped back into dialect when he had something important to say. I knew that, and waited), "tha' knaws these snails don't grow ev'rywheer. There's a dozen li'le beds o' cress upstream wi' never a snail on 'em at all. It's nobbut where there's lime in t' watter and this 'ere weed stuff where they'll stay."

Oh! That rather limited my scope. Still there *were* odd limestone trickles coming in. I remembered quite a few of them, even as I was soaking in George's remarks.

"So there are," agreed George, when I mentioned them; "and one or two more besides which lie a bit off t' stream like this one here. And them'll be t' best places, I'm thinking; they'll nooan get flooded so much. There's nivver a snail in this world could ho'd on in some of those spates that come down."

Well, that was true enough, too. I resolved to have a look at some of these places on the morrow. I dared not, of course, suggest that George leave his beloved garden altogether and come to help me to plant watercress; but at the same time he was obviously too useful a man to be wasting all his time up at the house, where I dined and slept and that was all. I did, however, tactfully suggest that he and I might have a walk up to some of these places when he had a little time to spare.

"Nay, there's never time to spare in a garden," he assured me. "There's always something or other to bother one. It's worse even than fishing!" I just caught the twinkle in his old eyes, and I knew that I had him.

"Tomorrow?" I questioned boldly. "First thing?"

"Aye; good as any time," agreed George. "We'll tak' a bit o' cress and some weed with us. What time d'you call first thing?"

I knew George started work somewhere about seven o'clock—he kept his own hours—and I was not going to leave a loophole for any sly digs about "t' day being half ovver by then". I looked him full in the face and said "seven oclock".

And seven o'clock it was, summer time. The sun

was just nicely up over the crest of the bluff at
Gurston Pot as we walked down together through
the dewy grass by the edge of the stream. George
had provided himself with a couple of buckets and
a good sized sack which he carried rolled up under
one arm. We loaded the buckets first; one with wet
weed, on which were huge masses of jelly-like
spawn as well as hundreds of mature snails; and the
other, half full of water, with as many of the
shrimps as we could get. This done, I held open the
mouth of the sack while George carefully took up
what roots he thought suitable. We packed these in,
not too tightly, draining off the water as best we
could, and soon we had it full to the top, part with
cress and part with weed. The sack was sodden, but
George recked little of this when I pointed it out.
He wiped it down a little with a wisp or two of hay
from the meadow alongside, and then over his
shoulder it went. The buckets fell to me.

I left the matter of suitable planting places entirely to him. He knew the valley from top to bottom, and he knew also just what I wanted. There
were little trickles almost everywhere; overflows
from the cattle troughs let into the fields; little runlets where the water was carried away from marshy
bits of meadow and pasture; tiny streams draining
miniature valleys of their own; there were a thousand

places. Some he used himself, clearing a little space between the rocks and gravel and planting a few shoots of his cress, or perhaps his flannel weed, and indicating to me where to plant others. In every one of them we put down a few snails or shrimps, or a bit of the ova jelly. We got on very well together, for I did not interfere with him. A few places he turned down altogether. "Floods," he explained laconically in some cases, "wrong bottom" in others. Twice we came upon sunken limestone-fed depressions similar to the one at Foggyshaw; and here George planted good quantities of both cress and weed; clearing out the exits, where it was necessary, so that the water, with its burden of fish-food, could make its way into the river. He put down the bulk of the snail ova at these two places, planting it in the quiet corners where a few tumbled rocks gave shelter. A wide patch of marsh marigolds, yellow and glorious in the sun, growing on a soft patch of ground draining into the stream, he left altogether. "Plenty of food there already," he explained; "it's nigh as good as cress for your job."

"George," I cried, "if you are sure of that I'd rather have them than cress; a thousand times rather." The thought of those great yellow flowers blazing by the side of my stream, delighting the eye and doing good at the same time, impressed me tremendously.

I think that one remark did more than anything I ever did to lift me on to his own level. Poor George; I believe that, up to then, he had classed me among the philistines who had no eye for beauty whatsoever. All the time since I had been back I had spent down by my river; building dams; talking, thinking, almost—he must have thought— living for fish. His garden he had deemed unappreciated. More than probably, indeed, he had long since come to the conclusion that I was one of those outside the pale who kept a garden as a matter of form. He looked at me with a new light in his eye.

"Then we'll have some," he remarked. He stood back and regarded the golden, glowing patch appreciatively. "They do look bonny, don't they?"

"George," I cried; "they're exquisite."

From that time on George was mine.

We planted cress and marsh marigolds in all the places where they would do most good. The hour or so I had begged of his time had long since extended into three or four. Twice we had gone back to Foggyshaw for more cress and flannel-weed; and many times had we taken a supply from other smaller beds we came across on the way up. "You'll maybe not get *snails* to thrive on all of 'em," George explained, dubiously, as he planted out his beds, "but they ought to be reight enough for shrimps. And at any rate they'll *look* well. And then", he added more brightly, "snails aren't t' only food trout feed on. There's a-plenty flies and grubs and things will nest on here and t' eggs hatch out. I reckon, if it comes to that, that trout will eat owt, wean't they?" It cheered him up remarkably, this thought. He could indulge his bent for landscape gardening untrammelled by the thought that the place he had chosen was unsuitable for snails. I honestly believe the day out did the old chap good. He was encompassing the destruction of his enemies —for I suppose all snails and such are enemies to gardeners—and extending his garden at the same time. I let him go on unchecked, helping him un-questioningly in all that he chose to do. The man knew what he was about; no doubt about that.

When I looked at my watch it was three o'clock. We had put in eight hours at it. Well, it was a good day's work. We had planted watercress and king-cups in places where they had never grown before. Every spot we had selected carefully, so that the beds would be free from floods and other dangers; and nowhere could the trout get at them easily to gorge themselves. The beds emptied gently, often over a little fall, into the main stream. There would be—or so I hoped—a steady, continuous supply of food; shrimps or snails, or perhaps both; always dribbling through to the pools below.

With the realization of the time came the sudden knowledge that I was hungry. We had spent the day providing food for fishes and had neglected to cater for ourselves.

"We'll slip up to old Bracken's for a bite," suggested George; "and then I'll take you to a place where there's a tidy bit of trout food doing nowt. We shall have to go up and see him in any case, 'cause I want to borrow a spade and 'barrer."

Bracken is another Scotsman. These dales seem to be full of Scotsmen or men of Scots descent. They say swarms of them settled here when Prince Charlie came south on his march to Derby. He sent a message back for a thousand pairs of brogues, and in course of transmission the order got misconstrued into ten thousand pairs of rogues. These came, by return, but I do not think many of them can have got past these dales.

We found Bracken himself in the hayfield; a big raw-boned fellow with a face the colour and texture of burr-walnut. He welcomed us with a vociferous bellow as soon as we passed the gate, and he carried on a shouted conversation with George all the time we were crossing the meadow towards him. Even as we drew nearer, and the need for noise diminished, he bawled away at us as loud as ever, interspersing his remarks with odd roars of laughter which sounded like a jovial thunderstorm. But he never stopped working. His rake flashed in and out in the sunshine continuously. A master-craftsman this; there were no wisps and but few strands left lying loose after he had made his stroke. The sweat was pouring down his tanned, good-natured face, but he went on working the whole time, talking to us in that great voice of his over his shoulder. We followed on behind him to the end of the row. There at last he did straighten up and look at us. "Aye, I reckon there'll be a bite o' cheese and some ale (he called it 'yalle') in t' house yonder. See t' missis. She'll tak' more kindly to ye by yourselves than if I came wi' ye. Ye might get a bit o' ca-ake then; but she'd nivver trust me at t' same table wi' it. T' barrer and things ye'll find in t' mistal, George. Tak' what ye want. I'll send young Tom over for them sometime."

He had started working along the next row even as he spoke. We watched him going along; the long brown arms shooting out with the steadiness and precision of piston rods. Haytime was no holiday for him. God-given weather such as this could not be wasted. At any time the great dark clouds could come rolling over the hills and for days and days and days there might be rain: or what was worse, a few odd hours of sunshine, half-drying the hay, and then more showers. Wet and dry, wet and dry, for weeks on end, blackening the laid out grass, depriving it of nourishment, robbing the dales of hard-won sustenance, making the crops in time hardly fit even for bedding.

Mrs. Bracken you have not yet met. She is a canny body. Small and plumpish, and with a tongue which wags unceasingly. We found her in the dairy with one of her apple-cheeked young lasses in attendance. Rich yellow pats of butter were spread around on all the whitewashed shelves. A clothes-basket full of eggs was on the floor. Milk was running through the cooler. It was very fresh and sweet and clean in there. She looked up with a smile at George's cheery "Good day, missis."

But there was no conversation allowed in there. We were gently shepherded into the house; and there on the big ash-topped table a cloth was laid for us. A huge boiled ham was given pride of place, and flanking it on either side a couple of tremendous pies. Then followed in quick succession pasties, cakes, scones, cheese, a score of things. The kettle was whisked off the hob and a scalding pot of tea put down in front of us. It was a meal for fifty people. And it had been got ready in as many seconds. Mrs. Bracken "mothered" us. A jolly little woman; she chattered all the time. I gave up trying to answer her questions—I suppose, really, she never expected them to be answered—and I sailed steadily along with the ham. George did rather better. He kept up a running fire of bantering conversation, speaking with his mouth full and as often as not with his china pot up to his lips as well. His old grey eyes flashed and twinkled unceasingly. George was enjoying himself.

I, too, came in for my share of chaff. Those dams of mine, and the work I had put into them, had not gone unnoticed. But I happened to be feeling a bit cheerful myself, after that good meal, and I gave as much as I got. I was almost sorry when George got up and started talking about his "spade and barrer".

There was no question of payment here; even my thanks were waved cheerily away. I had to wait a long time before I had a chance to reciprocate. Then, one market day I happened to see Mrs. B. in Badgerley. I rushed her off her feet and had bought her a new bonnet before she had realized in the slightest what I was about.

But, in the meantime, there is George, already coming out of the mistal with his barrow. The sun is still high, though the shadows from a row of sycamores now stretch halfway across the yard. From the next farm up the dale comes the endless rattling of a mowing machine, and nearer in, from a meadow not yet cut, the monotonous "crake-crake, crake-crake" of a breeding landrail. One of John's sheepdogs, a sleek, lissom little collie, comes fawning round my legs: while another peers at me through a tiny, square-cut hole in the door of one of the outhouses. A couple of dapper wagtails skip daintily here and there about the cobbles in the yard. Everywhere there is the scent of hay. High Summer in the dales: it is very beautiful.

But George? I caught up with George just as he was crossing the little arched bridge over the river. Of where he was going to I had no idea: some place where there was fish-food, wasn't it? Yes, that was it.

He took me along a cattle path through the pastures flanking the river, pushing his barrow along and chattering glibly all the time about the Brackens, their relations and their forbears, and I do not know what other light-hearted gossip about them. At a place where the river took a sharp right-angled bend, he pushed away from the stream as though to cut the corner. In a little dip there were half a dozen pit-like depressions full of reeds and stagnant water.

"Now look in there," demanded George. "*There's* some food for 'em if you like."

I did as I was bid.

The ponds were one mass of tiny, wriggling, bull-headed tadpoles. I looked at George in amazement. What did he intend to do with these? We could hardly dump them wholesale into the river. Anyhow, I hardly liked the idea of that—not that I have any great affection for frogs, but somehow it seemed such a massacre of the innocents.

But George already had his spade out of the barrow and was cutting a narrow channel between two of the ponds. "If we join these up", he explained, between strokes, "and then cut a gutter from the river there above the bend to the top one, and another from this bottom one back to the river again, we'd get a little current running through all the time. Some of these li'le taddypoles would be always in trouble then. They'd get washed down casual-like, just maybe odd ones now and then. He looked round him in mock consternation. "Begow, it looks like being one of Pharaoh's plagues o' frogs if we don't."

An idea struck me. "We can do better than that, George," I said. I knew that the next flood down would silt up his passages, even if it did not overflow them altogether. There had been a hundred yards or so of iron piping taken out of one of the water supplies up at my house; worn, thin stuff which ought to have been removed years before; and these lengths of piping were lying idle in one corner of the garden. Why not use these?

I explained to George how, if we did, we would have a controlled flow, whatever state the river happened to be in. As far as I remembered they were inch or inch-and-a-half pipes—just the size. He fell in with the idea at once. Another advantage occurred to me: we should not have an open gutter-like drain running across the bit of pasture; we could replace the turf afterwards and no one would know.

We dug out our channels deeper than originally intended; and then we both went up for the pipes. We could just finish before dark. The sooner we had the job done the better, for those tadpoles were already well-developed, and once they were at the frog stage there would not be many going down my pipe.

We got our pipe-line in without difficulty. One end we sank, protected from silting up by a tin can—that was George's touch—about a foot deep in a rocky pool of the river; and the other we laid so that it emptied into the highest of the pits. From there the current ran across the intervening little spit of soil into the next; and so on all through the five. We piped the final exit, turning it back into the river about fifty or sixty yards lower down across the corner. The fall was fairly sharp; there was a good flow shooting out of the pipe end almost immediately we had let the current through. We hid the outlet rather carefully, screening it as best we could among the herbage by the side of the river.

Just as a test, I held my handkerchief loosely over the end for a minute. When I withdrew it, a sodden little bag, there were two tadpoles in already.

It was a big asset, this new food supply. Snails, too, I thought might flourish in these ponds, and I mentioned it to George. My enthusiasm was quashed at once. "No lime," remarked he. "They won't grow without lime. And a deal of other things as well," he went on. "Funny things are snails. You find 'em where you least expect it; and where they ought to grow, they don't. I'm none so certain about these snails we've put in."

I was not going to have any depression creeping in just when I had made a scoop like this. I changed the subject at once. Lord knows what he might have said next. Casually informed me, perhaps, that tadpoles were out of season or something.

We walked home through the perfumed dusk. The smaller birds had ceased their songs, but from the moors above there still came down to us the long-drawn, bubbling cries of mating curlew. I stopped to listen, as I always do. It is the call all northern wanderers remember, wherever they may be. How many thousand times had I dreamed softly of some such night as this; with the last rays of the sunset's afterglow showing through the trees; and the pastures with the rabbits playing "touch"; and the browny-purple moors above; and the curlews calling. Calling, calling, calling.

Chapter X

Aesthetics

*

And now I come to where I made one of my
mistakes.

I had improved my river from a utility
point of view. Dams I had made: by the end of
August I had put in just over seventy. The food
supply—thanks to the watercress beds—I had increased immeasurably; for though I found that the
snails did not do so well as I had hoped, the shrimps
multiplied beyond all expectations. My tadpole
ponds still functioned; though the tadpoles had all
matured and were now, I suppose—what were left
of them—little frogs. Still, I left the tap running as
it were; and every time I passed I made a little bag
of my handkerchief and tested it. It was surprising
what a variety and multitude of insects came down
that pipe.

The extended water space, too, had undoubtedly
improved matters. As the summer wore on the
hatch of fly was amazing; and my thoughts de-

lighted in the remembrance of all the little gravel-beds I had covered—permanently covered. They should make good breeding places for many years to come. I watched, fascinated, the swarms of duns dancing up and down. Scores and scores of females were busy egg-laying over the shallows—*my* shallows; shallows which were never there before.

Those dams pleased me tremendously—as I say, from a utility point of view. I resolved to make them please me to look at, too. Even now, they fitted in remarkably well with their surroundings, for I had been careful to keep the character of my stream unsullied. There was nothing in the least *outré* or incongruous about those lines of boulders, strung loosely as it were across from one side to the other. None of them was straight or of even height: they dodged and wandered about everyway. There were a thousand delightful little nooks and crannies where fish could lie and shelter: as many streamy runs where they could feed. The sunlight, filtering through the bankside trees, made dancing patterns of light and shade on the rippled water of the pools. In the stiller places the overhanging trees, liberal of their fading glories, were reflected with a twofold charm.

I think it was the sight of these bushes which gave me my idea.

Aesthetics

All through the year, each time I had passed a certain pool I had stopped to look at it especially. One bank, whatever the season, seemed always to be a blaze of colour. A flowering currant, with its thousand little stars of purply-red, had I think first caught my eye. Immediately above, a wide-spreading tuft of forget-me-nots had made a vivid splash of blue; and then, perhaps ten yards higher still, there had been a dog-rose with its gay flowers lying like unmelted snowflakes on the green. Daffodils too: there was a bed of them just on the top of the hank which had been a glory in the Spring; and among a host of other things a hawthorn which I remembered to have been one mass of bloom.

Why could I not have all my pools like this? Pools which would delight the eye when fish refused to rise? Why not, indeed? Odd bits of stonecrop on the walls; wild hyacinths (though already there were many places where this flower grew); daffodils—there were a thousand plants which I could use; plants which would fit in naturally and not look as though they had been planted there. Not too many of them to start with; just enough. Just enough, I thought, to catch the eye; just enough to make each succeeding pool a fresh delight. And at all seasons of the year. That alone would obviate all chance of overcrowding or overdoing it. I would have little batches of flowers peeping out all through the season: as one died off another should be there to take its place. And all indigenous plants. Though many of those that perhaps I would use had never actually grown there before, I determined that not one of them would be of such a character that it never *could* have done so. I was not going to have my river looking like the ornamental waters of a municipal park. Transplanting of the natural wild growths—beautiful enough for anybody—would be the main part of the scheme.

The next spring I set to work.

The first thing to do, I cogitated, was to consult somebody who *knew*. George, of course, there was, but I did not want to be continually taking him away from his own work. There was plenty for him to do without helping me in what he termed my "whigmaleeries".

Almost at once I thought of him; a man with whom gardening, and especially rock-gardening, was a disease. He was the authority I wanted. He would tell me all I wished to know.

I rang him up. But the best thing he could suggest was to put me on to a landscape gardening firm. They were good, he said, very good indeed. In fact I imagined, from his description, that they might have designed Eden. He was still enlarging upon their excellencies when I was cut off by a long-distance call.

Now long-distance calls are unusual with me. There was only one thing that this could portend —trouble!

And trouble it was. I was required in London, urgently.

But, thought I, not so urgently but what I could break my journey as I passed through the place and see these wholesale gardeners. I could spend an hour or so there and tell them what I wanted. Then they could be getting on with it.

I hummed gaily as I packed. I was imagining how my river would look, perhaps not actually just yet, but later on, when all work would be finished upon it and I could fish. I was still humming when I drew up at the gates of the place which, from my friend's description, I imagined must be some sort of annexe to Paradise.

They took me in. I was given over to an enthusiastic youth in plus-fours and a cigarette holder who listened politely to all I had to say. I tried to describe what I wanted. Yes, he understood; a river— well, no, hardly a river—yes, yes, he knew just what I meant. What did I think of these? I did not catch the name, but they would grow over rocks and thrive—oh, of course they would thrive: all their plants throve, anywhere. And these? And these? He took me round in breathless fashion; and I must say some of the things he showed me were very lovely. I have forgotten the names of them all, or nearly all, but in the end I made a selection and sat down to calculate how many plants I would require. Just one or two, here and there, along the sides of my pools. The resultant sum rather startled me.

Then, as a second shock, I caught sight of the time. I had been three hours in that confounded place. I should have to hurry—more than hurry.

"Look here," I said. "I must be off now. Can I leave it with you? You know the sort of things I want—suitable for the banks of a stream and so on. When can you deliver?"

"Oh, tomorrow. We have our own vans, you know."

I wrote out my cheque. "Don't exceed that," I instructed, "and spread out the plants as far as they will go. Start at my lowest dam and work up. I do not know when I shall get back, but my gardener will show you where I mean. 'Foggyshaw Bottom' tell him, in case I have no time to write him. You understand what I want now, don't you?"

Oh, yes, yes—he understood all right. I need

have no fears of that. All through the seasons I should have flowers on my pools.

We parted with expressions of mutual esteem. I let in the clutch and left him to it.

Well, I forgot to write George; and I was away nearly a month. I met him in the garden on my return. I rather expected some reproachful glances —for after all, gardening was his province. But there were none. I had to ask him if the nursery-men had been.

"Aye, they've been," he replied laconically. "I started 'em in at Foggyshaw Bottom, same as they said you'd ordered."

"That was right, George. How did they get on?"

"Nay, I doan't know rightly. You see, sir, they wouldn't bide no interference from me. 'No,' they said, when I told 'em what I thought, 'we've getten our orders, and our orders we'll keep.'"

"Well, they understood what I wanted. It ought to be all right. Were they here long?"

"Three days. They stopped up at Mrs. Bracken's. I didn't see much of 'em. I was kept main busy up here."

"Mrs. Bracken would do them well enough. We'll have a walk down, George, after tea, and see what they've done, should we?"

"Aye, I'd like to come with you, sir—just to see, like."

I left him at that and went indoors. There was a note from the firm, giving me a list in high-hat language of all the plants they had put in—fifty of this; a hundred of that; and so on. I glanced at it casually. It was only the figures I could understand. George would be able to tell me which the plants actually were.

I found him waiting for me as I came out. "Now, George," I chirruped. "Come along and we'll see what those pools look like now."

The Foggyshaw dams, a series of three, are screened from the path leading down to them by a belt of trees. One comes across them suddenly, from below. I was chattering glibly away to George as we turned the corner. Suddenly all conversation ceased. I blinked. Foggyshaw low pool was a riot of colour. Every scrap of rock was covered by some wild, exotic growth which nearly blinded me. There were patches which looked like raw beef; others blue; some yellow; mauve; heaven knows what colours there were—*all* of them, I think. A tiny island—just a couple of rocks and some sand which I had left in the middle to break up the sur-face—had taken on the guise of a firework display. I suppose they had aimed at a floral fountain. And they had hit it plumb! My dam-wall had been lifted at regular intervals—about every yard—and on each little pinnacle a circle of small stones had been built, filled with soil, and a geranium or some such growth planted there. Twelve of them, in a row. I stared at them fascinated. A touch of a duller red showed at the base of one of them, and a wild suspicion shot across my brain. Good God; it *couldn't* be? But it was. Those twelve geraniums were in pots!

Avalanches of blooms fell gracefully over the rocks—floral waterfalls, I suppose—and every crevice seemed to have some sort of fern peeping coyly out of its recesses; just cocking an eye round the corner, as it were, and grinning at me.

The place made me dizzy. I sat down for a while. "Yes," I thought, when I had soaked it all in; "all we want now are a few mandarin ducks and a bag of bread."

I had forgotten George. When I looked up he was standing there gazing at a clump of lilies which formed a flying buttress to the dam. "What the hell, George," I commenced; but I could go no further.

He took out his pipe and slowly commenced to fill it.

"Nay, I told 'em what ye wanted, but they

wouldn't hev' it. Still, I'd no idea it was aught like this." He, too, relapsed into silence.

I rose heavily and stalked up to the dam above. This was quieter at the moment, but I could see that the explosion was already timed to begin. There were just as many plants as in the other, but they were only budding. In about a fortnight's time, perhaps. . . . The third dam, the last of the three, I calculated would be a month. I could see a bit more of the foundations here. A nice little path wound coyly up and down the side of the stream, with its border stones all proudly supporting some creeping growth or other. It led me to a little mound whose top had been flattened and the turf replaced. "A dam' good place to put a sundial," I thought—just like that. I dare say they may have thought of it first: it looked like it.

I set off for the pools above. I might as well see the lot; now the initial shock was over.

But the ones above had not been touched. There they lay, exactly as I had left them. So did all the others.

And then it dawned upon me what had happened. I had told them to start in at Foggyshaw bottom dam and work up. They had seen the three pools, one above the other, and thought they were the lot. My order for plants had been definite enough and they had put them all in. The seasonal flowering they had arranged by deciding that I wanted one pool to blossom at a time. Then when that was fading, the next came into bloom. And then the third. I remembered telling them that I fished there. They must have thought that I sat there on my backside like a Honolulu god, surrounded by flowers, and angled peacefully away until the plants faded. Then I would move up a score of yards to the next pool and sit down there for a couple of months or so.

I could see it all. And damned funny I should look, too! I had to laugh.

George added his mite of sympathy. "Well, there's one thing about it. T' next flood'll take 'em all out of sight, won't it?"

When I grasped what he had said I stared at him in genuine alarm. Of course it would; even the lightest freshet would rip up those plants like so much tissue-paper and bury them all down Gurston Pot. I couldn't have that; they had cost too much. Only the geranium things could go; they and their pots. I should love to see the storm water picking those up one by one and sending them to hell.

But then, I thought, sobering up, it isn't the geraniums' fault, poor devils. I could not blame *them*. "No," I thought, "we will use them somewhere." Another inspection and we would come to some arrangement, maybe. I couldn't now. I went straight home. Sufficient for this day, at all events, was the evil thereof.

The next morning, among my mail, was a letter from Ridsdale—the chap I had met at Raygill—asking me how my wire dams were getting on. My wire dams! I had forgotten them. Four pages he had filled with further helpful instructions; the result, apparently, of his own more recent experiments. A delightful, charming letter—so charming that I could not wait to reply. I telephoned him.

"My dear fellow," I pressed, "come up here and tell me more. Stay with me for a few days. Can you? Can you? At once? Oh, good!" Ridsdale. . . . Just the man I wanted to relieve my gloom. He would be here for lunch—as soon as that! I gave instructions right and left for his comfort. I was delighted to honour this great man. Towards noon I strolled down the road to meet him.

I found him parked by the side of the road just on the farthest outskirts of my wood. He had got out from his car and was gazing back down the valley. He turned at my approach and held out his hand. "Nice bit of colour you have there," he commented, turning back once more to look again.

"Send your car on up to the house," I suggested.

"We can walk and I will show you some more." A couple of words to his man and we were alone.

My wood interested him, as did the views of the valley as it opened out beyond the crags. He made me pause many times before we reached the house.

George was just through the gates. Ridsdale stopped and addressed some remark to him about the bed that he was working on. I saw George's quick look of approbation and the answering look from Ridsdale. No need for words between these two; they were friends already. In half a minute they were talking away—in language miles above my head—as hard as they could go. They went on for half an hour, wandering among the beds and with me trailing along behind. I did once venture a remark. Both of them stopped and stared at me. I think they had forgotten I was there. Then they went on and I wished I had not spoken. "Another gardening fiend," I thought. "Well, no man can be perfect." I buttonholed Ridsdale at last and told him lunch was waiting.

He laughed and turned towards me. "I'll be back in an hour, George," he said, taking my arm. "We'll talk about those Gesnerianas then."

Oh, *would* he? I wanted comrade Ridsdale to talk about dams, not gesnerianas. I got him almost there at lunch, and then in explanation of my delay in constructing the wire weirs I happened to mention my garden city down by the river.

I thought my friend was a quiet fellow. The way he laughed at my recital changed my opinion. "I must see this," he guffawed. "You have not altered it, have you?"

"George will possibly have salvaged the geranium pots," I said, "but he can hardly have done anything else. I only got back yesterday evening myself."

"I hope he hasn't," he remarked, "I hope he hasn't. I'd like to see the scheme *in toto* if possible." He hurried through his lunch to prove it.

"Come along," he said, as we both got up. "Where is this Foggyshaw you speak of?"

We made down to the gates. Ridsdale espied George pretending to be busy, but really quite obviously waiting for our return. "May we take George?" he inquired.

It was going to be my funeral this; I could tell that already. Ridsdale laughed whenever he looked at me. Well, George could attend the obsequies if he wanted to. I called him across.

If Ridsdale had laughed at lunch time, he fairly bellowed when I showed him my pools in actuality. He collapsed on to a tuft and literally howled with mirth. It made me ill to see him. Finally he looked up at me with his eyes swimming. "Where's the aspidistra?" he hiccuped. "Don't tell me they did not send you an aspidistra!"

I threw a clod at him.

"You know," said Ridsdale at long last, "come to look round, they haven't really made a bad job of it at all. Not by any means. Your instructions have been misunderstood evidently. If you can imagine this pool in a formal garden—lawns each side, and possibly some marble piece, which you didn't order, placed say there—it would look extremely well. Now, wouldn't it? Do this!" He showed me how to cup my hands so that they acted as a frame. "Now look through there," he commanded.

I did so. The backgrounds disappeared. All I saw now was the pool itself and its surrounding flowers. He was right. It *did* look extremely well. It would, indeed, look exquisite in the situation he had outlined.

"But planked down here," he continued, laughing once again, "it's . . . it's. . . ."

"We'll have no bad language," I remarked coldly. "What the hell are we going to do with it?"

He looked at me in genuine surprise. "Do with it?" he repeated. "We're going to put it right."

Chapter XI

Transformation Piece

*

O ver the next few days I will draw a veil. When I made my dams I worked hard: working under Ridsdale was sheer slavery. George seemed to love the job; and the man we got to look after the horse and cart liked it too, I dare say. But those two gardening fiends ground me under their heels. I felt like one of the old Israelites before Moses came.

All those tufts of flowering mosses, sandworts, stonecrops—I didn't know half their names—were lifted carefully and transplanted. Ridsdale did the job thoroughly. The first thing he did was to take a walk all the way up my stream, almost to Outershaw, making a plan of operations as he went. He took particulars of every pool, every bend, everything there was; and against each he pencilled little notes. In a couple of hours or so he had his scheme of operations accurately worked out. He knew just where every plant should go and he loaded up his

cart accordingly. He was director; George his fore-
man; and McNally—the man with the cart—and I
were labourers. We two serfs unloaded and carried
the soily, trailing masses across to George, who
planted them according to instructions, to an inch.
Some pools Ridsdale ornamented fairly heavily;
others he left with just perhaps one tuft. Continually
he made notes—possibly of my reactions under
stress.

Towards the evening of I think it was the third
day, just when he had got me into a state of exhaustion which precluded all opposition, he passed
me a note. There were a score of long-winded
Latin names on it, and against each a number.
"Order those," he instructed. "They'll cost about
fifteen quid. Get them from the same firm; they're
the best people there are, you know—or did you?"

It was the final stroke. What bit of resistance I
had crumbled. I ordered them.

They turned out to be shrubs when they arrived.
I thought, having paid for them, that I should at
least have been allowed to inspect them. But I was
ignored. Ridsdale and George took command and
all the conversation vouchsafed me was an order
not to touch. Each shrub—some of them were
pretty big—had its roots encased in a sack of earth
and half a dozen of them filled the cart.

I spent the next week or so digging. Ridsdale pegged a place and I dug a hole. Then, when he had passed it, I dug another. I moved ahead of them always; generally quite a few holes ahead. He and George and the man with the cart did the light work. For the first time I began to see the value of trade unions.

Towards seven o'clock on the Thursday—at least I think it was the Thursday; I had almost forgotten there was such a thing as Time—I finished the last of the holes and I went home. Where the others were I neither knew nor cared— somewhere behind, I supposed. But I had done enough. I was going back for a bath and a meal. Meals had been haphazard ever since Ridsdale had come: he had about as much idea of the etiquette due from a guest as a newborn baby. And if they wanted any more labouring done, they could hire it.

But it was all finished. They came back about nine o'clock. I was in an easy chair and I meant to stay there.

Ridsdale poured himself out a drink. "Had dinner?" he inquired, nodding towards the table.

"Um-m-m," I nodded back, staring at him defiantly.

But he had apparently done enough bull-dozing for one day. He just ruffled my hair as he passed out of the room and remarked, "I'll be down in a minute or two. Tell them I'm hungry. Mary will have kept something hot."

Mary would! That was just what Mary *would* have done! Everybody, male and female, seemed to delight in anticipating Ridsdale's wishes somehow. He had what my cook called "a way with him". The moment he entered the room again, there was Mary at the door with half a dozen dishes, piping hot.

He had me under the influence again, too, in five minutes. A dozen words and I was listening to his plans for the morrow with all my old enthusiasm rejuvenated; as keenly and as interestedly as though my back did not feel like a kidney-pill advertisement and my hands were not blistered and raw.

Wire dams: that was his programme for the morrow. The gardening was finished—"for the time being", he added, blithely.

"There is going to be no more gardening," I asserted. "All I am going to do in that line is to walk right away up the stream with you tomorrow and see who else besides myself has done any work. We will spend the morning at it, and then we will see about these wire dams as you suggested a moment ago."

"Sound idea! We'll decide where to put them as we go up."

I knew who would do the deciding, but I let it go. It was some consolation, at any rate, to think that for one morning at least I should be allowed to live like a human being. I thought I had better retire while he was in this soft and melting mood, before he had time to alter his mind and decide to build a road-house or something. I wished him good night and went to bed.

I forgave him everything the moment I saw Foggyshaw again. It was one of those glorious, clean, *English* mornings—sunkissed and radiant—when everything appears *alive*. We walked down towards the river by the bankside path. Overhead the noise of birds was everywhere; the trees were thronged with them; little, flitting, gaily-coloured shapes which dodged in and out among the foliage like so many jewels. Looking up through the branches even the undersides of the leaves were rich and luminous. Of darkened shade there was none; the shadows themselves seemed to be lit with yellow. The little stream laughed and bubbled as it danced its way down to the river. A gorgeous morning.

We rounded the row of trees, and my heart leapt across my chest. Foggyshaw lay there before me.

Foggyshaw . . . exquisite, entrancing, beautiful . . . so beautiful that it hurt. I stared and stared and stared. "Ridsdale," I cried; but I could go no further. I slipped my arm through his. . . .

Though the new plants and shrubs had been used sparingly, they seemed to fill the dell with colour. They had been placed just here and there, in the right places. They caught the eye, each one of them, and held it for a moment by virtue of their own loveliness. But only for a moment. Their greatest charm was in the way they led one's gaze to greater lovelinesses still; the way they opened up enchanting little vistas one would have missed before; the way they brought out the full beauty of my valley.

Foggyshaw, as I believe I told you, lies in a tiny amphitheatre of its own. A steeply-rising bank of trees lifts upwards from the little lawn which, on one side, slopes gently down towards the stream. Now, from out the vaulted darkness of this wood there flamed a flashing harmony of golden bloom, holding the sight in rapture for a moment, and then lifting it, almost unconsciously, to where the higher branches of a clump of pines made their own beauty against the sky. It was a beauty I had somehow never seen before. And beyond the pines, a little to the left, their bases shrouded in a pool of violet mist, there rose, as yet all hazy with the blue of morning, the majestic, craggy heights of Morraside Ghyll.

On the edge of the lawn itself there were two bushes planted; two only, each isolated. "Stenophylla" I was told they were. I do not know. All I saw was a falling rain of yellow stars glittering in the sun. The rocks by the stream-side had here and there a touch of unwonted colour; just a touch. But it was enough. It lifted them from drabness into sheer delight.

The other side of the stream he had even more lightly handled. Some little willows had been cleared from the bank-side: not all of them, just enough to break up too long a row. Now one could see through them, here and there, entrancing views of pastureland and meadow; pastureland all gay with buttercups and sweeping grandly up towards the spinney which crowned the rise. All the way round, on that side, one could see the hills beyond; lovely hills, all purply-brown with heather or grey-green with benty grass and bracken.

And that is what Ridsdale had done with all my pools. Each separate one held some utterly delightful feature of its own. There was not one that I could pass unheeding. At all of them I had to stop and gaze in wonder at the transformation that my friend had done. My river now was all a garden. There was not a plant too many—nor a one too few. They were a means to an end. All he had used them for was to bring out the high lights of the pictures which were there already. Each shrub had, in itself, an arresting beauty; but it was only part of the greater, all-embracing loveliness of the whole. The eye was drawn, insensibly, to what was there to see. It was all so natural; so carelessly done. But the apparent want of method was Method in excelsis.

We walked in silence almost all the way; for Ridsdale, too, loved all these things. His was the eye to have imagined them in the first place, but mine too could see their beauty when they were done. I came to the most distant of all the places I had made; a little dam, all by itself, away up towards Outershaw.

Here also he had worked. A row of hazels had been felled unmercifully; carted away and their stumps turfed over. The view upstream had opened out. I could see all the upper valley now in all its boldness; all its native grandeur. The stream came down through the park-like pastures which stretched away on all sides up to the hills. Those few hazels had, I saw now, just broken up the full majesty of the view. They had robbed it of half its character. Why, the wide skyline of the moors was simply magnificent.

"One would have had to climb a tree to get that view before," explained Ridsdale. "I tried all ways to use those hazels; but they spoilt everything."

I nodded gravely. I was considering how much I owed to this dear friend of mine. I was deeply moved. My river, always lovely, was now a thing of beauty almost beyond imagining. From head to foot it was the river of my dreams.

I turned as Ridsdale spoke again.

"Old Arnison took the trunks, by the way," he said; "that chap from Outershaw. Told me that if you didn't want them for making dams he'd use them for fencing. From the way he said it I rather gathered that he had got a bit of a joke on you about one or other of your building exploits."

"We'll go up and see him presently," I said unsmilingly. "But first I'm going to tell you something, Ridsdale—something in all seriousness. This river is yours—always—now and for ever—to share with me. There must be no question of . . . of host and guest things now. It's yours as much as mine." I looked at him shyly, for I am no good at that sort of thing. "I want you to know that, Ridsdale," I added lamely.

Transformation Piece

He slipped his arm through mine. "Let us go and see Arnison," he suggested quietly.

"But. . . ."

"I will come," he promised. "I will come whenever I can."

Chapter XII

Outershaw

*

Matt Arnison's dam! The one he had made months ago up at Outershaw by felling a tree across the stream. I had forgotten it; but now I remembered what a fool idea it had seemed; for the tree trunk was a foot under water and only an odd branch or two stuck out of the top. I remembered that he had spoilt what might have been a really excellent pool.

It had not been a joke then. I could be more complaisant now, with sixty or seventy dams to play with. An odd one did not matter. We walked on towards the farm.

Matt was at work dry-walling when we came up with him. Some of his less athletic Irish cattle must have made an error of judgment in their, possibly inspired, first dash towards the more fertile meadows of his neighbours. He greeted us gaily as we drew up with him.

"Just t' chap I was looking for," he remarked to

me familiarly. "I could do wi' a bit of help in this job; there must be nigh on half a mile wants doing up and down t' farm." He looked me over quizzically. "Ye ought to be good at it by now," he went on, "what wi' all t' practice you've had makking dams. If you'd promise to work as hard for me, by gow I'd set you on."

"While you went tree-felling?" I questioned suavely.

Matt laughed. "Ye haven't forgotten then?" he remarked. "I thought ye must have wi' never coming near."

"No," I said, "I've been too busy making dams."

Perhaps there was a little emphasis on the last word. He caught it anyhow. He grinned straight at me, and then carefully put down the stone he was holding on to its allotted place in the wall. "That'll do for t' time being," he declared judicially. "They'll none get over that unless they want to. Come on along to t' house. Missis'd like to see you about summat, I think."

The way up to the house, from where he was working, lay about a hundred yards or more wide of, and parallel with, the river from which we had just come. With the excuse that he wanted to look at one of his beasts, Matt led us back down to it and along its edge. It was a part of the stream I had not

bothered with—after that first abortive attempt—
and now I examined it more critically, in view of
possible improvements. As it stood it was just a
turbulent little beck with here and there odd holes
showing behind the boulders. A pretty enough
stream in its way, but very rough, very shallow. A
moorland beck; that was about all. Perhaps later. . . .

I saw Matt's dam quite suddenly. There was a
long, gleaming, brightly blue stretch of water lying
by the side of the pasture. It looked almost like a
lake, it was so big. I noticed Ridsdale's expression
quicken in interest, and the pair of us hurried on.
Matt was, for the moment, forgotten and lagged
behind.

The dam was high now; higher than any of mine.
Caught across the upstanding branches of the felled
tree lying across the bottom, were other smaller
branches, a length of railing, many sorts of drift-
wood. Upon these in turn had been caught all manner of twigs, grasses, turves, leaves—a thousand
things. The pressure of the water held them there;
nay more, it had welded them into a solid mass. It
dammed the stream effectively. The water poured
over in a couple of places only—both towards one
side. The rest of it stood high and dry. I could have
walked upon it almost, it was so strong.

It seemed a tremendous pool to me. The water

had backed up all the way to the top of the original depression. It must have been six or eight feet in depth at the deepest place, and it stretched, unbroken, far up the river; fifty or sixty yards at least. A magnificent bit of water.

Matt strolled up towards us. He was busy filling his pipe and his mind apparently far away. It was sheer affectation and I told him so.

"Oh t' dam?" he pretended. "Aye, this is t' dam we made. I was thinking of something else. What d'ye think of it?"

I told him that, too.

"Well, it didn't tak' long making, did it? Not so long as some of those others ye've been so busy with. It's what I always say: that it's only fools and 'osses that work. People that get on get others to work for 'em; even if it's but a drop o' river watter. I haven't done a thing to it since we left. It's made itself.

"And I'll tell ye another thing," he went on, boldly. "It's full of fish, too. I bet ye there's a hundred in it right now."

I could well believe it, after my experience with those others. Here was a dam twice, nay three times almost, as big. It would hold its proportionate quantity of fish, of that I was certain.

I turned to Ridsdale. He was gazing downstream to where the dancing, broken water dodged and trickled about the shallows. He agreed with me about the dam, however. It was a good pool.

Suddenly "silt" struck into my mind." What about a spate, Matt?" I asked. "It will silt up very badly then."

"Well, I don't know. Maybe little storms will make it silt a bit; but a big one won't."

"How is that?"

"Because it'll wash all t' dam lot away then; except t' tree itself, maybe."

"And the pool at an end, eh?"

"Nay, it'll fill up again as t' rougher watter finishes. As t' river goes down a bit, losing its strength like, there'll be other things catch on those branches and block it up again."

Ridsdale agreed. "Quite probable," he said. "The only thing to be watched for is sufficient firm shelter for the trout in the pool. I'd see that there were plenty of good big rocks and boulders rolled into it, if I were you."

"Plenty there already, sir," Matt replied. Matt, too, had apparently come under the influence! I, his landlord, never got "sir". But Ridsdale had it in five minutes!

It was true. I remembered the pool as it had been

130

before. The whole of the bottom was rocky; there was ample shelter.

"Well, that's all you want." Ridsdale turned once more to the downstream waters. "I think we'll put a few wire dams there," he said. "It looks ideal water for the job, and those gravel-beds certainly ought to be covered. They're magnificent breeding-stretches for fly."

"Right," I agreed. "We can start in whenever you like." I slipped into the dear, familiar brogue myself. "What is it t' missis wants, Matt?" I asked.

"T' missis?" he questioned, as though surprised. "T' missis doesn't want owt—unless it's a good talking-to now and then. How d'you mean, what does t' missis want?"

It had all been a plant to get us down to see his dam; to heighten the effect by surprise. However I was not going to be put off.

"Mrs. Arnison wants to see me," I asserted. "And if she doesn't, I want to see *her*."

"Is it some of her ale you're wanting?" asked Matt, with uncanny foresight; "because if it is, it's all gone. We had t' parson over last week and he took it for t' harvest festival." He turned to Ridsdale, but he was looking out of his eye-corners at me. "There's naught'll grow on this land up here, you know, sir; and we had to give him something.

I thought a gallon or two of ale would maybe be as welcome-like as a couple of onions." He paused a moment, and then: "It might bring in one or two of t' backsliders as well," he added, with another sidelong glance at me.

But I took no notice. I was striding away up the hill towards the farm. Outershaw is a typical old dales house, almost Elizabethan, and of softly mellowed stone, which still stands four square to all the winds that blow. A little grove of trees, bent over and only foliaged on one side, protect it a little from the gales. Byres and barns are also on that side; beautiful old barns built centuries ago, stone-roofed, and coloured here and there with many-hued spots of lichen. The grass all round is nibbled to a lawn-like smoothness, and a little beck of crystal purity comes bubbling down from the heathered moors immediately above. Of garden there is very little; just a plot of ground in front of the house, surrounded by a broad, low, dry stone wall. Here Mrs. Arnison plants out the few flowers which will thrive at this high altitude. For a couple of months in summer it is a mass of bloom; but for all the rest of the year it must be a struggle for anything at all to grow. The greatest glory of the place is in the beauty of its stone, and to me the most attractive part of the whole place is the courtyard at the back. Here the entire area is paved with random flagging put down centuries before any surburban gardener had ever heard of it; glorious old stones, all worn and mellowed by the passage of the years.

The walls of the house itself are time-softened, too; with oddly-placed long mullioned windows which are a pure delight. And over the door—a Tudor arch—there is carved no coat of arms; no crest—no, nothing of that sort. Man did not fling his pride about in that way up at wild Outershaw. "Here shall he see no enemy but winter and rough weather." That is what is carved above the door at Outershaw.

There were half a dozen lean, rakish-looking bullocks in the pasture as we approached the house. They stared at us coolly; not lowering their heads, as cattle do, and then backing stumblingly away. These waited until we were within a dozen yards of them, and then suddenly whizzed round and were off like so many deer. The leader jumped a low place in the wall, and the others followed in a bunch. The last we saw of them were the tips of half a dozen wildly-waving, upright tails as they made off down the hill. "That's reight," commented Matt, looking after them fondly; "that's reight. There's another gap in t' wall at t' far side. Keep straight on, owd lads, keep straight on.

There's better grass ower theer"—he chuckled wickedly—"and it's nooan mine!"

Oatcakes and ale; that is what Mrs. Arnison put before us; big, flat, wafer-like cakes of fine brown oatmeal, lifted straight from the drying rack above the fire and spread thick with butter. And ale—ale rich and dark and strong, a gallon of it; her own work, too. I laughed at Matt; laughed at him over the top of my tankard in his own big stone-flagged kitchen. "To all backsliders," I toasted, blithely.

"Backsliding ye'll be reight enough if ye have much o' that," said Matt. "All t' way home, ye will, where it's a bit downhill. It's t' missis's best, by t' look on't. I nivver see t' colour o' this brew unless there's company."

That ale certainly did taste exultingly good. Ridsdale put his pot down appreciatively. "It's got a kick in it all right," he commented.

"Aye now? That'll be t' strychnine likely. T' missis laces it wi' strychnine so's nobody can sup too much. I shouldn't try any more of it, if I were ye." He refilled his own mug as he spoke.

Strychnine or no, it was good ale. But it was powerful stuff. I soon appreciated the force of Matt's remark, and after a while we didn't "try any more". I reminded Ridsdale about those wire dams.

"Yes," he agreed, rising. "There's a likely stretch

just below Matt's dam. We'll have a look at it as we go down."

It seemed bare and uninviting enough water when we got to it; just a rough, boulder-strewn length with big, wide patches of sand and gravel at the bends. "We ought to cover those," commented Ridsdale. "The food supply away up here will be pretty small at best. We mustn't make the dams too high, either," he went on, after a pause, "for the fish will be running up for spawning later on. What about one here?"

The place he had chosen was some little way below a bend. Raising the water a couple of feet or so would flood the river twenty or thirty yards back and cover a belt of sand at least a dozen yards in width.

"Yes," I agreed, pushing a stake into the ground. "This looks all right. There is another much the same below. We'll have a roll of wire brought up and left handy."

Half a dozen sites we selected on that walk home, and after lunch we got out the netting.

"Stakes?" queried Ridsdale.

"All ready," I assured him. "George has them weathering, I believe, somewhere up by his potting shed."

We walked across to see. Yes, they were there all

right; twenty or thirty of them; and what is more, all heavily coated with bitumen up to within a foot or so of the top.

"Sound man, George," commented Ridsdale. "I bet *you* never thought of that!"

"No," I confessed, "I didn't."

I felt some qualms—needlessly of course, knowing Ridsdale's sense of the fitness of things—as to what these wire weirs would look like. I did not want them flung straight across. It would be a pity to spoil my river now.

But my half-formed fears were groundless. When we got there and had unloaded the coils of wire together with a few of the stakes, Ridsdale splashed into the water and took a piece of chalk out of his pocket. He marked outstanding boulders with a cross. "From here", he said, indicating a place on the bank, "to here, and then to here. Across to that rock, eh? And then down to that other. We could slope away from there downstream and curl back a bit as we near the side. That bank looks sound enough for stay-wires. What do you think?"

I thought as he did. There was no chance of incongruity the way he went.

"I've got George's tape here," he went on. "Let's see how much we want."

We wanted nearly twenty yards; and this length

we cut off, stretching it along the grass. "Never mind bending it yet," he ordered; "we can do that later. Give me a hand with these stakes."

We drove in George's stakes firmly. There was only a little water coming down, and but two of them which needed at the moment to be placed in the actual stream-bed. We did the best we could with these, diverting what bit of water there was, and digging out a couple of good, deep holes. Then we put in the stakes and tamped them down with stones. Both of them were very firm when we had done. The others we did in the same way across the dry part of the gravel-bed.

"Now for the wire-netting." One end we fastened very firmly to the roots of an overhanging tree, staying it with half-inch twisted cable both upstream and down. That end was fast, anyway. Then came the job of winding the netting in and out from stake to stake. We dragged it down from the upstream side, with its upper edge barely a foot above the water. It was fifty-four inch wire and a good three feet dragged actually on the bottom. Its meshes caught in everything. Unchancy, awkward stuff. However, it had no resistance, or very little, to the pressure of the water itself and we got it looped across in time. Ridsdale took up the hammer and a quantity of galvanized staples. He fas-

Outershaw

tened the top strand to every stake, and then bent
over the netting so that its upper eighteen inches
or so lay snugly against the post. Then he fastened
that. There was a foot of the wire perpendicular
and the remaining three or four lay more or less
flat on the river-bed upstream.

"A few good boulders now, to hold it down," he
remarked. For the next five minutes we were doing
that. All handy rocks and stones we pitched or
rolled on to this level flap. "That will do," at last
commented Ridsdale. "It won't be long before it
is covered over. Fits well into the bed of the river,
doesn't it?"

I was looking at that. The stuff was pliable
enough. It accommodated itself to all the holes and
unevennesses on the bed of the stream. The hedge of
netting stuck up maybe a foot above the surface of
the water and continued, at the same level, across
the sloping belt of sand and gravel until it reached
the other side. Already one or two wisps of grass
had caught and been held on the meshes. I could
quite see that, in time, a powerful—and yet natural-
looking—obstruction would appear here.

We made four dams up on the length below
Outershaw, and two more we put in a little farther
down. Half a dozen in all. They were quickly made.
They would silt up, I quite expected, but after all

that did not matter overmuch. I wanted these for fly-breeding more than to fish in. So long as they kept the gravel-beds covered I did not care particularly what they did.

I was to lose Ridsdale the following morning. He had been expecting a message for some time, and that day it came. We had breakfast and walked together down the road awhile. Then his car caught us up, and in another minute he was gone.

Chapter XIII

The New Cut

*

You will remember (or perhaps you will; it may have been one of the pages you have skipped), that I told you how, about half-way up my river, there was a fall some twelve or fifteen feet in height; and how above it there lay a bleak stretch of rock, over which the water swept in a shallow uninteresting sheet. That is when it was running normally, of course. All of it looked fine and bold enough when the river was in spate, and it was worth preserving for that alone. There was always something very fascinating to me in seeing that wild, brown, foam-flecked torrent go leaping over in a solid-looking mass and dash itself to pieces among the rocks below.

I had to keep it; no doubt of that. At such times it was the boldest, wildest bit of water that I had.

But the length above it? I had no use for *that*! Each time I passed it I disliked it more. I could not

see one sole redeeming feature in it from a fisherman's point of view, or—when I came to look at it
—from any other either. It had, compared to the
rest of the river, but little intrinsic beauty of its own.

What could I do with it? Even Ridsdale with his
flowers had passed it by. Once more I gave it up
and turned to move along upstream.

It was the sudden calling of a corncrake, I suppose, which was the root cause. Always when I had
wandered on from here, I had kept to the water's
edge; for just at this spot—save for a narrow strip of
turf—the river ran between high, almost overhanging banks, half broken rock, half grass and tree-
roots. I heard the corncrake calling from the meadow
just over the top, and I wondered if I could catch
sight of him. I clambered softly up the twenty or
thirty feet of bank above me and peeped gently
over. Immediately in front the land fell away into
a deep and narrow dip of about a dozen or so yards
across. Beyond it lay a level stretch of meadow
reaching back perhaps a furlong or more to the
boundary fence. The loud, monotonous croaking
ceased suddenly. My stealthy movement had been
detected. I looked all round but I could see nothing:
not the slightest movement stirred the grass anywhere. I waited a while, but it was no good and I
rose to go on my way.

The New Cut

Once up on the top, I kept there; walking beneath the line of trees growing on this narrow bank of earth separating the dip and the river. It curled and twisted here and there, this dip, and I found myself wondering how, in the first place, it had come there. Caused by the river, probably, at some time years and years ago: possibly at one time, in fact, the actual river-bed.

I pulled up suddenly. If the river had run there once, it could run there again! Where had it come in? I almost broke into a run myself in my eagerness to see. Yes, there it was, as plain as a pikestaff. Maybe thirty yards above the place where I had scrambled up, this old, forsaken bed curved sharply in. It was divided from the present stream solely by a narrow almost wall-like bank of earth and rock not more than six or eight feet thick. It looked almost as though it had been built purposely.

Downstream—where did it end downstream? I found that out, too. It finished up in a little marshy patch bordering a wide bay on the river; formed all one side of it, in fact. The bit of marsh I had seen, of course, many a time; but the banks of the dip were lower there, and I had never given them a thought; just passed them by as small unevennesses in the land.

But now! I would not pass them by now. I had my idea! One of Ridsdale's wire dams just above the fall, to cover over the unsightly rocks; and then a gap cut in the wall of the dip at the top end; that was all I had to do. And I would still have the fall in times of spate!

McLeod's land. I saw young McLeod within five minutes. In another five I had arranged the question of compensation with him—a small thing, this— and borrowed his spade and pick.

Quickly I got my levels. I decided just where my dam must be, and then I took a line—to decide what height it would have to be—from the level of the stream bed at the site of the proposed breach. I marked the exact spot on the bankside rocks above the fall. I did this carefully. I had to; for I did not want to have a stagnant pool forming between the dam and the breach; with, in times of drought, the possibility of a bare length of stream-bed showing in addition. If I kept the height of my dam above this spot I should be all right.

Then I commenced to dig. It looked a little job when I began it, but the impression I had made after an hour's work seemed plaguey small. The soil was inches deep only; all the rest was sand and gravel and a mass of boulders, all wedged tightly together into an almost solid mass. The soil—when I could get a shovelful—I flung back into the stream behind me; but I used the pick mostly. My thoughts turned longingly to a spot of gelignite; but I could not wait for that; and anyway it would probably have upset my levels, along with other things, completely.

All afternoon I toiled on; and towards sunset I had a way through. There was now a matter of six or eight inches only between the level of my gap and the surface of the water running by. That was all. I dug my pick down under the edge of the last boulder and gave a heave. It came away and a trickle of water ran through. The trickle grew. In a moment it had washed the remaining gravel away and almost all the stream was sweeping down towards the dip. The soil from the sides fell in, exposing more boulders, and my gap grew in width. The stream bed to the fall was almost dry.

"Good!" I thought, "good!" I clambered through the breach myself and saw the water slowly spreading down the dip. The grass was holding it a little, and in any case the level bottom of the place was fairly wide. All that had to be overcome, but it was a matter of an hour or so at most. Those fingers of water were reaching out in all ways. Soon they would touch the marsh and the way would be through. "Tomorrow," I thought. "Tomorrow I will finish it." I laid the pick and shovel under a tree-root and went home.

The New Cut

I took George with me when I went again; George and a length of netting and some stakes, both of iron and wood. I anticipated some difficulty in staking that bed of rock.

We could see the gleam of water long before we reached the dip. The nearer bank of the new cut-out was not hidden by trees as so much of the actual river was, and almost the whole length of it was enfiladed from where we were. It looked quite good; though the suggestion of wet grass was uppermost. Still, that was nothing. The first spate— not far away, by the look of the day—would alter all that.

We had a look at the gap first. It surprised me to see how much wider it was. The water had eaten away well into the banks. I had left it maybe a yard across; now it was nearer half a dozen. In depth, however, it was much the same. A big, flat ledge of rock lay most of the way across, and this I was glad to see. The erosion downwards was a thing I should have to watch most carefully if I meant to keep those levels in working order. I mentioned this fact to George. "Bit o' pitching will put that right," he asserted. "We'd better do it now, I think; and t' sides as well. Will it be wide enough, think you?"

Yes, it was wide enough. In fact it was just about right. The erosion had been stopped by two rather bigger boulders, one at either side; two boulders which, as they stood, would be useful as foundations for the walls. They were two good rocks: even as they were they would bear the brunt of all but an exceptionally high flood. We started pitching.

Diverting what bit of water there was coming down back to its late course over the fall was an easy job. We had that fixed in five minutes; and then we began to pave the sides and bottom of the gap. There were plenty of flat stones about, big and little. We cleared out all the loose stuff very thoroughly and wedged our stones in tightly. It was a neat piece of flagging when we had finished. George was insistent that we should make it strong. "Undermining," he explained. "Watter'll get under owt. Ye can't mak' it too strong. We ought to have had some cement." He looked round disparagingly. "Still", he said at last; "it'll maybe do. A spate watter will go straight on, mostly, and over t' dam. It'll maybe ho'd." He gave one last critical look at the stones we had put in—they looked heavy enough and firm enough to me to stand anything—and then he nodded towards the roll of wire we had brought.

"Better get on wi' it," he exclaimed. "It's going to rain hard by dinner time."

"Right," I agreed. "Come on."

Staking proved a difficult matter here. The flat ledges of rock which formed the stream-bed had but few crevices, and we had no means of drilling into the rock. One or two places, however, we did find; deep, narrow clefts which, full of water, ran down to a depth we could not fathom with any sticks we tried. A little manipulation and we forced two of the elm stakes into these and then jammed stones into the sides to hold them firm. One crack we found would take a couple of the iron, crowbar-like rods we had brought; and with these four we had to be content. The stay-wires, of course, we had no difficulty with; we could place those where we liked.

"Why not run a length of this 'ere stay-wire from side to side along wi' t' netting?" asked George. "It'll mak' it firmer."

"Good idea," I agreed, with my mouth full of little staples. "But we'll fix the netting first."

I clamped the wire on firmly; threading the meshes over the iron stakes, and hammering in my staples on the others. I did the job well. Then we tugged boulders—heavy, almost flat-sided boulders —on to the part laid on the bottom. And after that we ran a length of stay-wire in and out among the meshes and fastened it on either bank. The weir looked firm enough, but far from beautiful; for, unlike those others, this one went almost straight across. It was the only unsightly thing on the river; but it would have to do.

The rain was just starting as we left. By the time we had reached home a steady downpour had set in. The becks as yet had changed but little; but somehow one could detect an undercurrent of sound; a subtle difference in the muttering of the moving waters. It was as though one heard the flood gathering from afar off; a warning note sent to tell all who cared to listen of the storm water already in leash among the darkened hills. The grey sky looked as though it could rain for a week.

"Ah, well," thought I, "we'll see." My dams were strong. I had no fears for them. And this new job was sound. I went to bed content.

Chapter XIV

"Après Moi le Déluge"

*

I did not see my dams again for three whole days. It rained unceasingly; and though this, in itself, would not have prevented my going, I steeled myself to wait—to wait until the heavy floods which poured down in noisy, rushing cataracts from all the ghylls into the main stream, should have done their work. Then I would see how my dams had stood; how my newly-cut channel—the latest darling of my heart—had behaved itself. It was a trial, but I survived it.

Three whole days I waited, and then I went down through the sodden pastures to my river. All the dams had stood. They seemed unaltered, though I could not see far enough down through the dark brown water to judge the condition of the river-bed. Still; they were pools—that was obvious enough. I walked on rapidly up the river towards what I called the "new cut".

"Après Moi le Déluge"

The roar of the fall came to my ears while I was still a good way downstream. Water was going over *that* at any rate! As I drew nearer I had qualms about the safety of the wire dam that we had thrown across. There seemed to be such a roar of falling waters. I looked round the banks as I progressed to see if there were any signs of its disintegration.

And then I came to where my new channel emptied. I saw the swirling water shooting out between its banks; marshy now no longer, but clean-swept and wide. My diverted stream had scoured out a channel for itself. All softer earth had gone. It was down to bed-rock and, where it met the original main stream, it had gouged out a deep, tormented pool. Heavy water was coming down here, too.

I could not cross either stream. I had to work up on the outside of the fresh passage. The more I looked at it, the better I liked it. In places it was a dozen yards across. Rough, high boulders lined the banks; and every here and there, tall, jagged pinnacles of rock thrust themselves out of the flood. The water must have carved out a pretty deep pathway for those to show: there had been no sign of rock three days ago, when I had looked across that dip for the first time.

"Après Moi le Déluge"

I tried to visualize it as it would be in normal times. Good, I thought, extremely good. I could imagine attractive eddies forming behind those rocks; could see, in my mind's eye, all manner of swift runs and quiet corners by the sides of them. Already, in the slowly falling waters, I thought I could make out where they would be.

On I walked, delighting in the promise of this new toy; and at last I came to the place where George and I had made our gap through the bank of the main stream. We had builded well. There did not seem to be a stone displaced, and the two high rocks at either side had stopped all chances of erosion. The water had risen high as it forced itself through between them. I could see where the level had been; for all underneath it the bits of soil which had filled the tiny crevices in the stone had been swept away. The water poured across the sill in a swiftly moving sheet, breaking up into yellow, swirling foam as it met and broke upon the rocks and boulders just below. Looking at it from up here too, this new length was a most attractive piece of water.

And my wire dam above the fall had stood. I could just see the heads of its four stakes above the water. Then the level of the stream seemed suddenly to drop a little; go on again; and finally disappear; dark against the clouds of spray whirling upwards from the pool below.

As a matter of duty I went on, right up to Outershaw, examining my dams. They had all stood. As I went higher the water cleared a little, and I could make out the bed of the stream. Silted up at their bottom ends some of the pools undoubtedly were; but in every case the fall from the dam above had scooped out a compensating depth. The wire weirs Ridsdale and I had put up were splendid. Tree branches, twigs, grasses, turves, hay—all manner of things—had lodged against them. The wire sagged between the stakes at times, but that was nothing: it held. They made attractive dams, too; for there were places here and there across the width where some bigger article had lodged and now stuck upright, breaking up the level top line of the weir in most attractive fashion. In others the grasses and such-like light things had been swept away as soon as they reached the top of the netting. Water did not pour over everywhere in a level sheet; it broke through just here and there and came through fast. In the corners, where the netting was fastened to the banks, great masses of stuff had gathered, and against these heaped up piles a yard or more thick, quantities of sand and gravel had been swept, forming little promontories jutting out into the stream.

Turves over those, I thought, and then. . . .

But it was my new channel I thought of most. All the way downstream again I thought of that. And when I came to it once more I spent an hour there, delighting in this thing that *I* had made; this water which was *really* mine. I had *made* a stream, myself. That was the burden of my song. I had turned part of the river and made a good place from a bad one; made two streams out of one. I was full of it.

I wondered if there were other places I could use. But no; as I wandered on downstream I could think of none; though I cast speculative glances here and there in hope. I found myself toying with grandiose schemes; such as, for instance, once when, just above Foggyshaw, I halted upon a high, bankside bluff to look upon a view which always captivated me. Across the river the bank was high too, though not so high as the one I was on, and beyond it there lay a wide, marshy hollow in the land which was wholly unreclaimed. Too low-lying to be drained successfully, it had just been left; a big, rough, plover-haunted pasture all clumps of reeds and tufts of bog-grass, wonderfully varied in its form and colour. It stretched away until the rising ground which bounded it changed the character of its herbage. On one side pastureland sloped gently down;

green slopes of grass all dotted with the brown shapes of cattle and divided up into a chequer-board of hedgerows. Straight opposite, four or five hundred yards away, a broken bank of woodland rose steeply, almost from the marsh itself, sweeping round to join the trees of a little ghyll which, in its turn, formed the boundary on the right-hand, downstream side.

Could I but run a passage round the edge of this marsh, I thought; what a lovely length it would make. I thought of limpid pools lying under the lee of those attractive pastures; and wild, dark depths below the broken limestone scars and towering trees of the wood; a wood which, I knew, was a maze of bluebells in the spring. That bit—that bit above all—would be a glorious stretch indeed. I could see it plainly.

I pulled myself together with a laugh at my own foolishness. My thoughts had run away with me. There would be a mile of digging here; not half a dozen yards! And even then, I calculated—in my right mind once again—what sort of stream would it really be when it was done? Slow and monoton-ous probably; even if it ran at all; no water for me, at any rate. Why, the marsh was almost flat! I called myself a fool and carried on the little way I had now to go.

"Après Moi le Déluge"

No more rain came. The next day the river was almost down to normal. I went once more to look at my "cut-out", and its promise of yesterday was fulfilled. I could see plainly now. A hundred little pools had formed, and between them the stream tossed and bubbled gaily round and over the clean, new-looking boulders of its bed. It was a joyous, happy bit of water and made an easy passage for any fish wanting to get up.

The wire dam above the fall had held up well. It still stretched across quite firmly and was now a dam in very truth. The branch of an elm had fallen and been washed down until its upper portion lodged against it; the thicker, heavier, trunk-end had caught upon the bank some yards above. It broke up the hard line of the wire, with its masses of held-up rubbish, and made in fact a most attractive corner. The water appeared to have been dammed effectively. It stretched back as far as the gap I had cut, in one unbroken sheet; vastly superior, I thought, to the bare, flat, rocky ledges which had been there before.

I went back down the stream very pleased with all that I had done. Little improvements would suggest themselves later. I would let Ridsdale see it first.

"Après Moi le Déluge"

And so, once again, I came to the marshy pasture. As usual, I stopped. The little length of river just in front of me seemed singularly unattractive now—after the happy, purling brook that I had made—for just here, for just this particular fifty-yard length, the river happened to run straight and quietly. Above and below I knew it was as near the heart's desire as one could wish; but, as I say, these odd fifty yards I did not like. I was still hankering, it appeared, subconsciously, after that imagined length round the edge of the marsh and beneath the wood yonder, five hundred yards away. But this thought I fought down resolutely. It was absurd.

Still, I thought, harking back to the river, surely something could be done to improve this? I looked up and down that straight, canal-like fifty yards with something approaching disgust. A wire dam? No—for even then, the pool would still be feature-less. "Featureless" was the word I was after. I wondered how I could put some feature, some bit of character into it. It was too straight as it was—too sober. I wished there had been a break of some sort in its sides—a bay or something; even a bend.

Well, there were at least the makings of a bay at any rate. The high bank which bounded the stream on the far side—a rather artificial-looking bank it was; for it was only a yard or two wide, dropping down quite steeply again to the marsh on its other side—curved sharply back at one place, and between it and the river lay a wet-looking bit of land half-covered with wild rhubarb. A dozen yards long, this bay would be, by as many wide. It might make a decent eddy sort of place—if it were dug out deep enough!

Digging! Everything seemed to be digging! I appeared to have spent half the summer digging; what with Ridsdale's holes, and gaps, and things. I resolved to put Matt Arnison's precept into use. If I could turn the water into this corner it would soon be scooped out. Well, thought I; a groin would manage that. If I built a groin well out from this side it would direct the flow straight across on to that bed of rhubarb stuff. I would scour it out.

Right. I set to work.

Of boulders there were a-plenty on the bank side. I started in twenty yards above; sloping my groin down and across towards the hole I wanted to clean out. I made it strongly, for I wished the whole force of the water to play on it. Higher and higher I piled the boulders; thicker and thicker; so that not a drop of water would be wasted. I must have rolled and tugged many a ton of rock and stone into position; more than perhaps was necessary, I dare say, for as I went on I found that the rough dam I was making helped considerably in itself to break up the monotony of the length I objected to. And it certainly altered the flow of water. I could see this gradually veering over and working out the soil even as I progressed. One plant after another was undermined, fell and was washed away downstream.

I seemed to be making a better job of it altogether than I had expected. On my side of the bank, the water below the groin, instead of draining rapidly away downstream, remained there; and, before I had finished, here too the water was circling round in a most attractive eddy; shallow at the moment, certainly, but it would gradually deepen; that I knew.

Well; that, too, ought to help matters. It had done so already, for I no longer looked on that length with the same disfavour. It was broken up quite nicely even now. And, of course, it would soon be better: the next flood would clear out the rhubarb and its mud-bank completely. I should have a good, big double-eddy; two well-sheltered places where trout would lie without a doubt. A few of Ridsdale's plants now, just here and there, and the job was done.

I put on my coat well pleased.

The idea of these groins rather interested me.

There were quite a few stretches on the river where, it came to mind, they might help to break up a too level bit. Why, I thought, by means of these I can dodge the river in and out of the banks as I think fit—scoop out curves—make new gravel-beds—there were all manner of little alterations I could make in the nature of the stream. And those eddies were *good*! Yes, thought I, we must have some more groins.

But I would wait a little until the water fell somewhat: with trying to work in its present state I was pretty well wet through. Tomorrow, perhaps —if there were no more rain. . . .

As a matter of fact there was. The heaviest rainfall of the year occurred that night. Occasionally one does get sudden storms away up in these hills; storms when the rain comes down in torrents, flattening everything it strikes. Our little rivers are dangerous then. The sudden addition of any heavy mass of water is apt to burst the bogs and marshes on the moor, releasing all the pent-up water of perhaps six months or more. And it does not come down gently; one can hear the roar of its approach some distance away. It is good that it is so, for on several occasions I have known of its approach only by this means. Overhead there has been a glorious sunny sky; the fells alone being dark and cloud-capped, with perhaps just odd streaks of lightning flashing down through the blackness. Miles away the storm has seemed; so distant that the thunder has been but a faint and intermittent rumble. Then, above the sounds of birds and the laughing cadence of the water, has come this sound. A minute afterwards—perhaps less than that—a wall of dark, menacing water has come tearing down the stream with the speed of a racehorse. There is generally just time to wade out on to the banks and clamber into safety, but one has to be quick. The sudden flood comes racing on; and what was ankle-depth a few moments ago is now a wildly raging torrent six or eight feet deep and in which nothing at all could live. Great boulders, a ton or more in weight, are tossed and rolled about like marbles; trees are uprooted; railings ripped out and smashed to matchwood; sheep and cattle drowned. It is rather awe-inspiring to see one's little beck transformed, almost in the twinkling of an eye, into a maddened flood which would do credit to a big and powerful Highland river.

There is flooding of the meadows, of course, but this is generally lower down. In the higher reaches the banks are steep, cut out deeply by generations of such storms as these. It is this confinement which

makes the water rise so quickly; makes it so dangerous to the unwary fisherman, wading as he may be
in what, a moment before, was a peaceful little
stream, perhaps even a foot or so below its normal
level.

Such a storm struck my valley that same evening.
We in the lower reaches did not get it so badly; but
all the hills were screened by an inky pall of darkness, shot through and through with blinding stabs
of light which flared and passed and flamed again.
The air throbbed and pulsated, even so far away as
this, with the echoes of the thunder reverberating
among the crags and corries of the fells. Outershaw
—Outershaw with its bit of 'As You Like It' above
the door—one's thoughts flew continually to Outershaw. They would be getting it. One saw the need
of the welcome in such times as these. May there be
no poor wayfarers seeking shelter on those wastes
now!

A flood we knew there must be; but never such a
flood as this! I stood at the window of my house
and watched it. In half an hour the river appeared
to have risen half a dozen feet: a fast and dangerous
torrent which swept everything before it. The roar
of its passing almost deafened me, even here. Again
and again my thoughts shot to my dams, and then
on to Ridsdale's plants and shrubs. Most of these he

had planted fairly high up the banks, well above the reach of all normal flood; but this . . . this looked like spoiling everything. If it went on another hour I knew that there could be nothing left. But surely by now—I thought; I hoped—every moss-hag on the moor must have been burst and washed away: there could be no more pent-up waters to come down; just the rain itself. Rain I could allow for; it was the extra water which made me afraid.

I stayed there at the window watching the flood until the darkness crept down and hid it from my view. I fell asleep with the roaring of the waters in my ears.

"By gow, tha's done it now, Maister!" were the first words which greeted me as I put my nose outside the door on the morning following; a lovely sunshiny morning, with the air clean and washed and fresh, and great white galleons of clouds sweeping full-sailed across the blue of the sky. "By gow, tha's done it now. Look yonder!"

I followed George's outstretched finger down towards the river above Foggyshaw. Over the intervening trees I could make out a great, wide sheet of water, blue as a sapphire and with gay whitehorses galloping merrily away down all its length —a lake which, to me, seemed to spread over half the valley—a vast expanse of white-capped waves which stretched away far out from the river until it met the woodlands where the hill-slopes began.

"Hell," I cried, and set off running.

It was on the far side of the river. I splashed across the stepping-stones below Foggyshaw and galloped on up the bank of the stream. The deep-cut gorge of Borra Beck I took almost in my stride; sliding down its near bank and clambering up its steep farther side on hands and knees. As I reached the top I halted dumb. Spreading out on all sides in front of me was a wide waste of wind-swept water. The marshy pasture—five hundred yards by three, in places, I dare say, four hundred wide—had gone. Its reeds and rushes showed up at the edges, that was all. Three islands, little tree-girt eminences, stuck up in a clump towards the middle. All the rest was water; save only, of course, for the high bank I stood on and which ran all down the ghyll side and then turned off—a narrow wall of earth now—by the edge of the main river back towards the place where it had been breached.

I made my way slowly along this bank, and then on until I came opposite my groin. Farther I could not go. It was the groin which had caused the damage. As George had said, "I had done it now!"

"Après Moi le Déluge"

I had builded far too well. All the storm water had
been turned and shot directly on to the soft earth of
the bank bordering the rhubarb bed. A breach had
been inevitable. It would not take long; practically
the whole force of the river had been used as a
battering-ram. There was a gap almost the length
of a cricket pitch, through which the water was now,
very slowly, draining back into the gradually falling river. But this running-off process would not
go on for long. It was very shallow over the sill of
the breach—six or eight inches, no more—and as
soon as the level had fallen this little way, no more
water could escape. The low-lying pasture seemed
to be permanently flooded. Unless, of course, one dug
out a channel away downstream, almost where the
bordering ghyll came in, and let it empty that way.

I strolled downstream again to see just where this
gap would have to be; but when I got down towards the place I examined it but cursorily. It was
a dull job looking where to make a hole in a bank
with all that glorious sheet of sunkissed water
spread before me. For it *did* look glorious. From
the high bank where I stood I could see the whole
great stretch of it. It ran all the way up the river-
side, divided from it only by a narrow strip of bank,
upon which odd trees showed here and there, until
it met a slope of higher ground away on the far side

of the marsh. From here the edge of the water ran, with many bays and inlets, along the foot of the pastureland, and so on round until it seemed to lave the bottom of the bluebell wood I had so longed to use before. The sight of that quickened me once more. I hurried on to make sure. Yes, I could see it now. That bank of cliff and woodland dropped almost to the water's edge. There was a strip of land only twenty or thirty yards in width between them. And that blue water, in that setting, looked simply exquisite. I climbed higher up the bank to have a better view. From here too, as I turned round, I could see it all—the whole wide sweep of it—with the river beyond and the park-like meadows and pastures beyond that. Farther over still, the sloping "intakes"—half grass, half heather—rose steeply up towards the browns and purples of the moor. And then, highest of all, glorious in its grey-green livery, smiling down on all my valley, with the dark cloud-shadows playing hide and seek across it, was the great, crag-broken mass of Morraside Fell.

I sat there for a long, long time. No, I thought. I could not let this go. It was far too great a gift to lose.

I rose in full determination to go and see my tenant farmer now, at once, and make the best arrangements that I could. But first, I thought, I would climb a little higher and look down on it all again. I set off; clambering up towards the higher slopes of the hill. And as I walked it dawned upon me that when the river fell to its normal height there would be no more water coming in: this lake whose new, fresh beauty so appealed to me would become a stagnant sheet of water; drying up, it may be, during long dry spells. I could not have that.

Naturally my first thoughts fell upon the ghyll at my side. I would have to turn that in somehow. But how? There were no banks here that I could cut through. The stream had just dug out a deep and narrow passage from the rocky ground itself. The land on each side sloped upwards, ever upwards. It was part of the moor itself.

"Now, Maister. What's 'ta think o' yon?"

I turned round, startled. It was Jim McLeod with a brace of sheepdogs at his heels. He had come up behind me as I stood there gazing down, wondering how I was to keep this lake of mine. He was smiling at me out of clear, grey eyes.

"Nay, Jim, I don't know what to think. I was on my way to see you, but thought I'd have a look round first." I gazed down soberly into the valley far below. The lake lay like a sapphire set in jade. Neither of us spoke for some little while. "I want to keep it, Jim," I said at last, turning to look at him.

"Well," he smiled. "That'll be all reight. I never used yon pasture much: it was always too wet and rough. Though, by gow," he laughed, "it was never so wet as it is now. Ye built that groin very well!"

"True enough, I did. But I didn't expect this!"

"Och, it's no great loss," he soothed me. "T' rent on it is practically nowt, ye may remember. It's always been sort of chucked in wi' t' other land, as ye might say. We're not going to fall out about that. It'll recompense ye a bit, maybe, for what ye did for t' missis. Begow, she's rare set up wi' yon stove ye've put in for her. There's hot watter day and night for her now. Sakes! If I told her we'd been arguing about yon wet bog she'd bite the face off me."

All my worries sped away. "Leave it to me," I commanded. "And," I added in all sincerity, "I'm very much obliged, Jim. But now look here. You may be able to help me. I want to keep that lake and stock it; but from what I see there is going to be no more water going in until the next flood comes down the river. I'd like to hold the level about where it is, if I could. I was wondering about this ghyll, but I can't see any place where it can be turned in."

"Come on wi' me," said Jim. "There's a spot

near half a mile farther up. Let us have a look at that."

Half a mile! This glib, long-legged dalesman talked lightly of half a mile. Of digging! What did he think I was—a contractor?

But I fell in beside him all the same. We strode boldly out between the heathered banks up the bed of the stream. Higher and higher we rose, until at last we came across a big, wide amphitheatre of marsh. The stream ran down one side of it, draining slowly through the clumps of rushes and bog-grasses and then pitching down over a little fall and away down the ghyll. Jim drew my attention to a re-entrant on the opposite edge of the marsh. Here, at one spot, the surrounding slopes of heather and peat seemed noticeably low. We skirted round towards this dip and climbed the bank. It was only a few yards thick and a second bit of marshland lay on its farther side. From this seeped out a tiny trickle which meandered gently away down a wall-side. It was very small; one could trace its course only by the greener verdure at its side. It wandered quietly down; ending, I suppose, in one of the little field-drains coming out into the river somewhere near the ghyll.

"Now, Mister," explained Jim. "If you're wanting a supply of watter, why not cut through this bit

of a bank and turn some of the beck down that way.
There's a spring or two in that lowside bog already,
and as you see, a li'le drop of water running down.
It comes out just by t' far side of the wood, you
know. You'll have happen seen it; but it's very
small, even there; more like a drain than owt. Still,
that's t' way it will run, if it'll do."

Do? Of course it would do! I could not wish it
better. The bluebell wood, with a stream coming in
by the side of it. . . . Why, it would be Paradise.

"It won't affect your pastures, or anything?"

"Not a bit," he assured me, blithely, "not a bit."

"Well I'll cut it through tomorrow. I'll bring
George up with me."

"Nay, I shouldn't bother. I'll be round here after
my sheep. I'll give you a hand. It's nooan a big job;
the stuff's soft."

"Right," I agreed. "I'll be up about ten in the
morning, or thereabouts. Will you bring the tools,
or should I?"

"I'll bring 'em," he said. "And now I must be
getting on. I got some sheep ower at Kirby market
last week, but by gow they're more like homing
pigeons. I've nobbut found half of 'em."

"Good-bye, Jim," I cried. "I'll be up tomorrow,
about ten."

I was up there at ten; but the job was done.

McLeod must either have been there soon after dawn or else be a miniature steam shovel. He had a gap cut clear through the bank of peat; a dam thrown across the stream which split the current into two; and a channel dug through the marsh which guided one half of it straight across towards his cutting. There was nothing for me to do except look down upon the little brook which now wound merrily away, tinkling and laughing, down the hillside towards the lake. It was a feeder, a good one, for—apart from the beck water—the springs would always give a small but steady, permanent supply.

Well, there would be generous compensation for him this time! "Jim," I said, "I'm going to pay for this. It would have taken me all day, probably more."

"Nay," he protested. "It's nowt."

But I was not having it. I let him see it.

"Well now," he remarked, at least; "there's one thing I *would* like. T' missis would be reight suited if I could get it for her."

"What is it, Jim?" At that moment I was prepared to give him anything he asked for.

"Well, I'd like yon spare Light Sussex cockerel you've gotten ower at Foggysha'. Begow, he's a grand 'un. He'd. . . ."

"He's yours," I cried. "And a pullet or two with

him." Fowls! He could have had *all* my fowls! George looked after quite a few of them, I knew, but my interest centred in one bird only—a mixture of all the breeds created, I should imagine. "Biddy," I called her, and she had the best hackles on her that I have ever seen. I shikared Biddy myself fairly regularly; not for eggs—which did not interest me—but for feathers. If Jim had asked for *her*, I might perhaps have made some little reservation. But as it was . . . Light Sussex . . . he could have the lot!

"I'll see George," I said. "He'll bring them across tonight."

"Well, it's real kind of you, sir. It's nowt that I've done for ye, really; but t' missis. . . ."

"Get after those sheep, Jim," I cried. "I'm going to follow this beck you've made right down to the wood."

Chapter XV

Guests

*

You must have had enough of my river for a
while. Suppose I tell you, for a change, of
some of the guests who came to stay with
me. It is the rainy season now; and though I myself
am one of those who believe that all weather is
good weather, perhaps you are more sensible.

For I had guests, you know, even that first year.
I have already told you about Ridsdale; though, to
be sure, no one ever seemed to think of *him* as one.
He was "the boss" with everybody, myself in-
cluded. Anyway, he is part-owner, though he will
admit it only when I corner him. Alas; they were
not all, they could not be, like Ridsdale.

The first fisherman who came, I think, was old
Morrell. Years and years ago he had been a house-
master at my school, and somehow, in all my
wanderings, I had kept in touch with him. I wrote
to him when first I landed back in England, and

then again, a little later, when I found that my dams held fish. He would be very aged now, I realized; though still, I knew, in his dry veins the old deep passions would yet glow; a gentle flickering, perhaps, in place of the old flame; but doubtless still the same unsullied, virgin fire.

He came to see me; a dry and wizened little figure, looking at me speculatively through thick-lensed glasses. The boy he had remembered had grown up. I think that then, for the first time, he came to realize that no longer could he claim to stand *in loco parentis*.

But he still did. He always will do. Dear old Morrell.

That night, in the quiet hour after dinner, we went out on to the lawn and this courtly old man showed me his household gods. "Do you remember this?" he asked, handing me his old greenheart rod. "It is my favourite still, though it is growing old now. Let me see—how old? Thirty—forty— why, I must have had it nearly fifty years. It has served me very well; for though I have had other rods, I have loved this one the best, always." He raised his tired old eyes to me almost apologetically. "We know each other so well, you see; this rod and I. We have grown old together."

He replaced it gently in its case, and his flybook

came out; an old, worn, pigskin case, mellowed and darkened by the years to almost the colour of mahogany. He handed it to me to look through. "I cannot make my own flies now," he went on, in that quiet voice of his, "though there are many there that I *did* make. That is the best of hair, is it not? It never perishes.

"Yes, those are my dressing. It is a pattern I got from a great friend of mine; he himself sent me the feathers from New Guinea."

I looked at the page of flies; little, tiny, feathered things, exquisite in shade and workmanship; every one a labour of love, undoubtedly. I passed on understandingly. March Browns—Dark Snipe—Woodcocks—a little host of patterns; all beautifully made: all neatly arranged in rows; tail-flies and droppers; and on the fly-leaves between the felt pages, each name was written in that wonderful copperplate hand which now, with so many of the old things, seems to have completely passed away. "Light Needle; Dark ditto; Dotterel & Yellow. . . ."

"Not a proper Dotterel," he hastened to explain. "I would not have a dotterel feather in my book. I use a starling." He peered at me softly over the top of those thick glasses. "Are you still interested in birds?" he asked. "I once spent a whole vacation watching dotterels up in the Grampians. They let me stroke them; actually stroke them. Most confiding, trustful little birds. I could not bear to think that I had benefited by their death. And they are rare now, you know. It is very sad. It is very sweet to have a wild bird trusting you—don't you think so?"

I nodded, just speaking now and then, while the soft and gentle voice went on, telling me of his friendship with the birds and beasts and wild things he had met everywhere. His erudition was profound. He told me things—life-histories of all the river flies we used—how I could distinguish the different songs and call-notes of birds—oh, a thousand things—gossiping happily away to me, while the low sun sank slowly out of sight behind the darkening fells.

I gathered up his kit and led him indoors. The night air, even in July, away up here is chill to old bones. "Tomorrow," I suggested. "Tomorrow we will take these flies of yours down to my dams and try them. Should we turn in now, or . . . ?"

"Yes, I will go to bed now. It is late enough. Will you awaken me, for sometimes I sleep deeply. . . ."

I nodded soberly as I led him to his room. One time, I thought—only too soon now—that sleep would be a little deeper, a little sweeter. . . . He would pass gently, dear old Morrell; pass gently in his sleep . . . from one stream to another.

I placed his rod carefully in my rack and locked it up. His flybook I took upon my knee again, fondling once more the flies that he had made; wonderful flies, exquisite in their workmanship and form; all on hair; beautiful, level, transparent hair which I think he must have had for years.

"Are you not going to fish?" he asked me as we set off the following morning. I had slung his creel loosely over my shoulder and I held his landing-net.

"No," I smiled, as I handed him his rod; "not today. I am going to ghillie for you."

"But that is very kind of you," he agreed, patting my arm gratefully. "I really must confess, though, that I do not care to be alone too long. I am very old now, you know—eighty-three last February. It is a great age. And I cannot see to put on my flies so well—you will be useful there!"

I nodded smilingly. "Up or down?" I questioned. "Would you care to start at the bottom and work up, or. . . ."

"Oh, downstream, please. It is easier for me—now."

"Right," I said. "We will run up towards Outer-shaw and send the car back. Come along."

I started him on a streamy pool up where the Stonebeck comes in. His long, fine line, with its cast of hair and tiny hackled flies, curved gently out and fell, as softly as its own shadow, just where the rougher water ended and the ripples began. He might have been fishing with a cobweb. The three flies just seemed to float down. One sensed the master, the indisputable master, at once.

Nor had we long to wait for proof. I do not think his tail-fly could have travelled above a yard before I saw his rod point go down and he was busy with a fish. Very softly he played it—exactly as I should have imagined this gentle old man *would* have played it—coaxing it, more by persuasion than by any effort of force, into the quieter water at the side. I crept down with the net and brought his capture back to him; a goodly fish, as fat as butter, of well over the half-pound. He examined it as it lay in the bottom of the net. "Very beautiful, is it not?" he said. "Can you take the fly out for me?"

That was no trouble. It was held by the merest bit of skin. His strike must have been like lightning; the lightest touch. I saw why immediately; for as soon as the hook was free he took the net and its fish away from me. "Should we put him back again?" he asked; "or do you want him for the table? I myself never eat them."

Back he went. This was a man after my own heart.

And so we went on. He had remarkable sport; and this, I am sure, was due wholly to the gentle way in which he fished—that, and the quality of his tackle. The water was dangerously clear, even for upstream fishing. It was a revelation to me, the command he had over that supple, almost willowy rod, with its fine, thin line hardly thicker than an ordinary gut cast. And then that ten-odd feet of horse hair! He dropped his flies exactly where he wanted, to an inch; curving them round obstacles, dodging them between the boulders. It was a re-markable demonstration.

"Do you always fish downstream?" I inquired.

"Yes, now I do," he answered. "It is easier for me and, in spite of what the textbooks say, I really think it does not make much difference. One must keep rather quieter, perhaps, but then, it is pleasant to be quiet, don't you think?"

I nodded. I did think so.

"And dry fly? I suppose you never use dry fly. . . ."

The quick eyes glanced at me sharply. There must have been some slight inflexion—wholly unintentional—in my voice. "You're not one of these confounded purists, are you?" he barked.

I was shocked. Such belligerent tones from my dear, gentle, old friend startled me. I stared at him, I should think, for nearly half a minute. "God forbid!" I cried, at last. "Why?"

"I thought you might be," he remarked. "So many of the younger school are. But take it from me," he went on, tapping my arm to accentuate his words, "there's just as much skill and vastly more knowledge required in good wet-fly fishing as ever there was in dry. I've tried them both. I know. One can't just wait to see what hatch is on with wet-fly fishing and then put up an imitation. You have to *know* what fly is on, even when there's not a sign of one to be seen.

"And you can't go by books, either," he continued, still belligerently. "I think the most absurd stuff is printed in books. They give you a list of March flies; then April; and so on. Are all our seasons the same? Why the biggest hatch of March Browns I ever saw was in June!"

I listened intently. The old man had reeled in his line to talk to me. He was the dominie again. He had something to say.

"You'll never become a wet-fly fisherman unless you study," he went on. "Things in nature work together. They are all closely affected by the weather. The swallow doesn't arrive on the same day every year, does it? No, of course it doesn't. Neither does the iron-blue dun hatch out on the same day every year either. But the two of them arrive together. If you see your first swallow hawking up and down the river, I warrant you will see your first iron-blue soon afterwards. It may be early or late in the season. As I tell you, it depends on the weather.

"And it's the same with other things. The smoke-fly comes out with the plane-tree leaves, though they are quite independent of each other individually. Did you know that? Or that the sand-fly came with the willows? No? Well, that's the sort of knowledge you want."

He snorted as he once more drew off line and started to fish again. "A List of March Flies," he grunted, evidently quoting from some publication or other. "March Bunkum!"

"Eighty-three years old," I thought. "He's wearing well."

But he was a master of the art; there was no question of that. For sheer accuracy and softness of casting I had never seen the like. Fish after fish he hooked, played and landed. It seemed to make but little difference in what water he dropped his flies, whether it happened to be in the quick, rippling runs or on the quieter water of the pools. He moved very softly along; there was no excitement; no wild striking. The tiniest flicker of the rod top and a fish was hooked; caught purposely, I am sure, by the merest fraction of skin. He intended to put them all back; and he meant to put them back unharmed. Nor was this just out of consideration for my little river. He did it everywhere. I found out later that on all waters he almost always came home "clean". And yet everyone knew that, as a fisherman, almost everywhere he went, he stood alone.

Three days he fished; three very happy days. "I have enjoyed my stay," he told me as, at last, he bade me farewell in his train at Furrowfield. "You have been very patient with an old man." His shaky, thin, old hand took mine. "Good-bye," he said, "good-bye. I shall not have time to forget your kindness."

I bent to arrange his rug and cushion for him in the corner of his compartment. Dear old Morrell. As I drove home my heart seemed very full.

Bennett, Firth and Dutton came to see me next. They came all together, just as I was going in to lunch. They had been fishing up in Cumberland, and when the Eden rose in spate they called on me; as Bennett said, "to save hotel bills".

"How long are you staying?" I asked. I thought I would be as hard-faced as they. "The bar is closed for repairs."

"Why, has Firth been here before?" asked Bennett.

"I shouldn't be surprised," I answered. "Though of course he wouldn't necessarily mention it to me."

"You'll remember th-th-this v-v-visit, anyway," shouted the maligned one. Firth stammered rather picturesquely, by the way. He took a flying tackle at my legs and the pair of us came down on the grassy border of the rose-bed. He picked me up by coat and trousers—incidentally he still plays forward for his county—and bumped me up and down. "Is it p-p-pax, you old d-d-devil?" he barked; "is it p-p-pax?"

I tapped the grass three times. "That m-m-means three stoups of ale," he explained. "It's a c-c-code we have. One for me and one for thee," he carolled, "and one for. . . . What are you chaps going to have?"

I led the way indoors.

I knew these three. I had known them far too long. They say there are no gentlemen in the wool trade and I am beginning to believe it. I almost emptied my cellar before they were sober enough to think about food.

"Does himself well, doesn't he?" commented Bennett, as we sat down. He lifted a cover. "What the hell?" he exclaimed. "Truite à la plume de la gardener's son! Do you mean to tell me there are trout here?"

I nodded.

Firth butted in. "We've brought rods; got any m–m–maggots?"

"Only three," I answered.

"You're seeing double," said he. "Dutton's only half one." He glanced across at him. "But, Gad, can't he eat?" he exclaimed. "Just stop and watch him a m–m–minute. I must congratulate your cook," he remarked a moment afterwards. "These t–t–trout are very good. How old is she?"

"Wesleyan," I told him.

"S–s–salt, please, Dutton," he commanded.

Then Dutton took up the tale. He had been overshadowed before, but now he had time and to spare. Those other two were children to him. "Heard this one?" he commenced; and he repeated it at minute intervals for a solid hour. I spilt my coffee on the carpet and, when I could, I cursed him roundly.

"Now, about this f–f–fishing?" began Firth, as we

made a move outside. "Bennett, if you and Dutton will take the top half, I'll work up to you. I shouldn't take a creel; p-p-put them in a bottle; I want some spinning-bait. . . ."

But both Dutton and Bennett were busy with their rods; split-cane, powerful rods; rods Diana might have fashioned. They had them up like lightning. These too, it seemed, were proficient at their art. I strolled across to them and laid hold of Bennett's. It was a heavy rod, and the dry-fly line he had put on was heavy too. I moved towards the open space of lawn. "By all means," he agreed, as my eyebrows lifted in question. "Chuck for those aquilegias." Those aquilegias were about thirty yards away and I laughed. I got out about twenty and was satisfied. "A nice rod," I commented.

"How do you know?" he snorted. He took the rod from me; pulled off half a dozen yards more and shot the lot out in a false cast. Still a further half dozen yards, gathered off the reel as his line swept back behind him, and then once more it flew out towards the aquilegias. The tapered cast at its end seemed to hang for a moment over them, and then fell softly down across one outstanding bloom. Thirty yards at least it must have been. I turned my head to speak my appreciation. Even as I did so another line flickered out, whizzed back, forward again; and there, touching the first, was another tapered cast. A couple of yards behind us stood Firth, grinning at my surprise and already reeling in his line. "E-e-easy," he commented, airily. "Ask Dutton there."

But Dutton was busy with his flybox. He selected a tiny midge-like dun and tied it neatly on. He handed the furnished rod to me and took my arm. "Come along," he suggested. "We'll leave these ribald devils. Where did I put that net? Oh, here we are. Now let's see what *you* can do."

He and I made our way down the stream to Foggyshaw. At the head of the pool were three or four fish well on the feed. I thought I would take the nearest one and moved upstream towards him. "Try him from here," suggested Dutton, laying a detaining hand on my arm. "You see; you'll reach him easily."

Surprisingly enough, it was so. The heavy line put play into the rod. I had nothing to do except direct my fly. In fact I cast two or three yards ahead of where I had intended to. But it did not matter. I saw the golden gleam of a second trout as he turned, and a moment later I had struck and was coaxing him downstream. He fought hard; but it was too much for him. There was no doubt of the issue at all; at any time.

I did not greatly care for it and handed the rod back to Dutton.

He understood. "All the fun in the casting?" he remarked. "Eh?"

I nodded.

"You're quite right," he agreed. "After all, these rods are made for heavy fish. The best fun I have had with them has been with sea trout. We went up north for that, you know; but the spate came and we made for home. It was Firth who remembered you had a place somewhere out here."

"I'm glad he did," I laughed. "Come along; I'm interested in this casting."

"Useful on a big river," he remarked; "but here. . . ."

The line curved out before him as he spoke. His fly dropped jauntily almost on to the nose of a rising fish. That, too, was brought quickly downstream. And three more besides. The accuracy of his throw was simply marvellous; for the pool that we were on was overhung with trees and every other cast had to be made almost underhand or round a corner. Here was another master of the art, though in a different style. And a master who could teach his pupil. I spent a profitable afternoon. The five fish we had caught were good ones and I kept them for the table. All others we put back. I got my share, for Dutton was keen to teach me all the tricks he knew. These new and powerful rods were fresh to me; and the command of line they had went rather to my head. They were no good for my trout—that I could realize of course—but the actual casting with them was a sheer delight.

And later on, when I had made my lake, I found that it was useful too.

We met Firth and Bennett just below Woogill, walking back downstream. They looked at me, I thought, with a new interest. I was anxious to hear their criticism, for they were both fishermen of some repute. I could go by what they said. If they were only serious enough to say anything sensible at all!

But they were honestly impressed. "You have a lovely little water here," commented Bennett, looking round him in genuine admiration. "If I'd brought a lighter rod, I believe that I should have asked to stay."

"Why, aren't you going to stay?" I asked, disappointed.

"Not this time," he replied. "Not this time. Wool Sales tomorrow you know." His hand dropped on my shoulder. "But it's been good to see you again, and to see what work you are doing here. We shall need all the fishing that there is in time to come.

Our sons, you know . . . and *their* sons. . . ."

I parted from these friends, too, with sorrow. They had brought a whiff of boisterous good-fellowship along with them which swept like a sea breeze through the quiet loneliness of my valley.

It had swept through my cellar, too. I stood amazed at the quantity of ale they had consumed.

I forget whether it was some little time after this, or if it were just before—yes, it must have been before—that I received a letter from John Packington; or Sir John Packington as I found it was now. He had progressed since I knew him. I remembered him as being keen, even in those old days, on geology and such-like things, and his letter bore this out, for it was a request for permission to examine, at length, the caverns in Morraside Ghyll. I recalled that somewhere in the background there was a wife and daughter, and—it is my way—I was fool enough to extend my invitation to them also. I happened in the course of my letter to mention how busy I had been trying to improve the length of fishing that I had.

And this, I think, was my undoing.

They came, the three of them; driving up in a flamboyant car which they promptly sent back home again. Packington himself; his wife, Lady P.;

and their daughter Pamela. The two womenfolk appalled me. Pamela might have sat for the model of a post-cubist painter, and her mother, Lady Packington, was one of those big, strong, horse-faced women with a loud voice and the smell of the stables never far away. She was visibly annoyed at the state of the road up the valley, and looked down her nose at the arrangements of my garden. "Why don't you try ranunculoides instead of this?" she demanded, kicking up a little tuft of creeping-jenny with the side of her number eight brogues. "And that helianthus wants pruning. Doesn't your man know?"

This was within a couple of minutes of her arrival! Her daughter was trying to look coy with a Mme. Herriot to her lips. Packington himself was busy gazing up at the limestone crags of Morraside Ghyll, which showed, blue and hazy, a mile away, above the trees.

I turned to him. "The caverns are under those cliffs," I explained. "I will take you up. . . ."

A harsh bark sounded at my ear.

"I understand you have some fishing hereabouts."

I turned to find that fiend at my shoulder. She was staring superciliously at the beck flowing past the end of my lawn. "I hope *that* isn't it?" she questioned.

I began to detest this woman. "No," I replied, shortly. "That isn't it." I looked at her again. "Thank God," I added.

But the point was lost. "I should think so, too," she responded. "What about lunch? I'm almost famished."

We went indoors; and as the meal progressed I saw her taking stock of everything there was: food, service, napery, everything. She made no complaints however. Perhaps she was wondering what sort of an adversary my cook—were I only wise enough to arrange the meeting—might prove. Martha, in her kitchen, was sure of her ground. She knew in what affection I, and everybody else, held her. She knew her work was good. I began to wish, with a perfectly fiendish glee, that this woman Packington would make some suggestion about the cooking. There was Viking blood in Martha; Viking and Scots and Irish; Yorkshire dales blood and I suspected the possibility of Welsh. A tough mixture. Martha was afraid of nothing on God's earth, save that, perhaps, some pudding might "set-on".

I tried to work it, but the woman would not rise.

"Home-grown," I commented, wickedly, the memory of those ranunculoides strong upon me, as I helped her to some strawberries. "We grew them. . . ."

"Really?" she interrupted. "They are very good."

Damn her.

She got her rods out immediately after lunch. "Think this is light enough?" she sneered, whipping an eight-ounce fly-rod back and forth through the air.

But I got a smack in there. "We've only trout," I exclaimed in mock apology. "The salmon cannot get up so far. I use a little four and three-quarter ounce thing myself. We don't get many fish bigger than about three pounds." I spoke casually, off-handedly on purpose. She stared at me; but I was quite at ease. I had not lied. We *don't* get them above that weight. In fact I had never seen one above three-quarters of a pound. But I did not mention that.

"What do you generally fish up here—wet or dry-fly?"

I thought I'd be high-hat for once. "Oh, dry of course," I asserted, with glib inaccuracy. "One doesn't. . . ."

"M'mm. That's rather unfortunate. I've only wet flies with me. I thought it would be all this chuck-and-chance-it business up here. I'll borrow one or two of yours, if I may. Where do you keep them?"

Guests

She helped herself when I showed her. And to casts as well. She took enough of both to last her for a whole season. Then she filled her case from my cigarette-box; had a last look round to see if there were anything she had missed; and then at last set off for the river. I watched her until she was out of sight, striding down with those great feet of hers; her rod waving above her head in figures of eight and every now and then a cloud of smoke floating upwards from her cigarette.

Pamela was reclining, all legs and lassitude, in a garden chair. From under a picture-hat she had dug out from somewhere she rolled her eyes up at me until there was little but the whites to be seen. It made me feel quite sick. I made a hurried excuse and went to find Packington. I had last seen him chipping out a fossil from one of my window-ledges with a geologist's hammer.

I found him still there, still chipping, though at another fossil.

"This Morraside Ghyll," he questioned; "do you know if it has been explored thoroughly?" "Never," I lied gaily. "I don't think anyone has ever been above a hundred yards or so from the entrance."

"But it goes in farther? . . ."

"Oh yes," I cried. "Oh, undoubtedly. I should rather imagine the caverns are very large."

His eyes lit up with the enthusiasm of the pioneer. "I wonder if you would be so good as to show me them now?"

"Of course," I agreed. "That's what I've come along for. Have you got a torch or anything—and some string?" He was not a bad chap, old Packington. When I thought of his wife and daughter I felt he was entitled to a little consideration. I tried to make things easy for him, even if it should be only for a little while.

"Yes," he answered, carefully feeling in his pockets. "Yes; I have everything I need for this afternoon. It is just a preliminary survey I wish to make, you know. I will start serious work to-morrow."

I thought that possibly by tomorrow I should have started in on serious work, too. My brain whistled every time I thought of that horror down by the river. And that other in the garden. . . .

But old Packington; I took him to the entrance of the caves; told him to be careful; and sneaked back home by a roundabout way to avoid the lawn.

We met again, all four of us, at tea. Packington himself had fallen into a pit half-full of water; stagnant water which he thought had contained a number of dead bats. I gathered he had had some difficulty in getting out again. Pamela had rolled her eyes about so much that they had become tired and she had slept. The three of us watched Lady Packington come striding up the pastures from the river.

"I'm afraid this stream is not much good to me," she exclaimed, nastily. "Haven't you got anything a little—er—should we say 'less adolescent?' Look at these!" She opened her creel and exposed to view half a dozen average sized trout, most of them just over the quarter pound.

I looked at her under drawn brows. "You should have put these back," I lied, severely. "They're undersized. Why didn't you?"

My shot told. She looked uncomfortable. I tasted power, and like a fool I tried to use it. " 'Three pounds' I told you," I went on. . . .

A sudden shriek of laughter made my teeth grate. "Three pounds?" she yelped. "Do you mean to tell me that there are fish in that ditch weighing three pounds?" She laughed at me once more, like a horse.

"Will you have some tea?" I inquired, coldly.

The more I thought of those three-pound fish the more I realized what a fool I had been. Suppose she challenged me to catch her one—me, with my little four and a half ounce rod! I seemed to have over-

Guests

done things somewhat. I went for a stroll into the garden to think things over. I could hardly plead pressure of business as an excuse, because I hadn't any. A sprained ankle suggested itself as the best way out; a sprained ankle with plenty of bandages.

I ran into George, just tidying up round the tool-shed. I thought that he perhaps might be able to help me.

"George," I asked, "do you think Martins in Furrowfield will have any three-pound trout?" Martins were the biggest fishmongers I knew.

"Martins?" said he. "Nay, I shouldn't think so." He took a couple of draws at his pipe. "But I know who has."

"Who, George, who?" And then, without giving him time to reply, I told him of the predicament I was in.

It seemed to please him. He slapped his knee appreciatively. "Now I know just t' chap," he assured me. "Old Fred Brocklesby down at Bishopside." (Bishopside was Lord ——'s place, a few miles down the dale.) "He's got a stewpond hidden away up in t' woods yonder with some fish in it which must weigh nigh on to five p'unds apiece. He feeds 'em up like chickens. And when his lordship and t' other gentlemen have been fishing all day and copped nowt, they just ask old Brocklesby to go out and get 'em a brace or two for t' table. Well, Fred, he just reckons to get out his rod and he goes and yanks a couple o' four-pounders out o' t' stewpond with his net, and he's back at t' Hall with 'em in half an hour. Begow, he's a rare reputation as a fisherman has old Fred among t' gentry as knows him. He nivver lets on, of course, how he gets 'em. If anybody asks him what fly it was, all he says is 'a li'le black 'un'."

"And would he let you have a brace?"

"Aye, that he would. Him and me's old mates. I'll get 'em for ye any time."

I clapped him on the back. "I'll let you know, George," I grinned. "It will be some time to-morrow, I think. This job wants some thinking out."

I walked back to the house in high glee. What was the best way to work it? I meant to have those fish there at the proper time. They should have their entrance centre-stage—with all the lights full on.

At dinner I started to reconnoitre.

"Are you going to fish tomorrow, Lady Packington?" I inquired, during a lull in the conversation.

She looked at me coldly. "I would like to run over to the Weatherheads' tomorrow," she remarked. "They have a length on the Ribble. Will you be using your car?"

Guests

"No-o," I said, doubtfully. "What time will you be back? Before dinner?"

"Oh, sevenish; I suppose. I never fish after about five o'clock. . . ."

"Best time!" I interrupted, blandly.

"Oh, do you think so?" she snorted. "But then of course things are different here. I must try it some time."

"Do," I responded.

The subject changed.

"George," I said, next morning, "I want three good big fish leaving at Foggyshaw Foot about seven o'clock to-night. Can you manage that?"

"Aye, of course," replied George, as though surprised at the question. "Will you be there yourself, or should I leave 'em? There's a hollow tree just by t' dam you made; they'll lie snug there until you come for 'em."

"They'll do there splendidly, George. You'll fix up with Brocklesby, won't you? And then I'll. . . ."

"Oh, that'll be all reight," scoffed George. "Him and me's mates. Seven o'clock they'll be theer. Three grand 'uns!"

And so they were. I spent a day of torture entertaining Pamela. Packington had gone to his caves, and the job fell full-weighted on to me. I showed her roses, and she gushed free-verse at me: suggested tennis, and we played pat-ball for an hour. Then she posed gracefully until lunch; looking at me under lowered, flickering lashes when I spoke and raising them when I didn't. I grew to hate the sight of those great blue globules with their underlying rims of white.

After lunch she thought she would like to learn to fish. "Can you cast?" I asked; "at all?"

"Oh, yes; a little," she replied; but it was a lie. Not even a little. I had got out a rod and reel and let her try. Well, I went on with it. I demonstrated and explained; demonstrated and explained. Then I took hold of her elbow to show her how. She liked that. The lashes flickered at me more than ever.

"Oh, how silly of me", seemed to be a favourite phrase. She referred to herself, of course; but it applied to both of us. I realized that to the full. I think, in the end, we got out about five yards. Then she said that she was tired. "I don't think I should ever have patience to fish," she sighed, subsiding languidly into her chair. I looked at her. Patience! Good God!

We called for tea; and Packington, moderately dry this time, joined us. We dawdled round until about six-thirty; and then I picked up my rod and casually, quite casually, remarked that I would just have half an hour's fishing before dinner.

Sir John pulled out his watch. "What time did your mother say she would be back, Pamela? Seven, wasn't it?"

"Oh, I'll be back before then," I interrupted cheerily; fixing on, for their possible remembrance, a tiny little midge fly to my cast. "I'm only going for half an hour."

The fish were laid there when I arrived; three lovely great fish, the smallest of them a good three pounds. I dipped them in the river and laid them on some wet grass in my creel. Then I sat down, my eyes glued on the distant curve of the road where it came out of the wood by Gurston Pot. I could not be seen, but I could see.

She was on time. It was not quite seven when I heard a horn and saw my car come sweeping out between the trees. It disappeared towards the house and I started on my return.

The others had joined her. All three of them were on the little strip of lawn outside the porch when I hove in sight and crossed towards them.

"Good sport?" I inquired, as I came up.

"Fair," she replied, throwing open the lid of her creel. There were five fish there, averaging about a pound. She did not deign to ask me what I had done. The glance she threw towards my tiny rod was enough.

It was Pamela who peeped into my basket and let out a screech. "Oh, and you've only been away half an hour," she giggled. "How perfectly *marvellous!*"

"What's marvellous?" barked her mother, elbowing her daughter aside. Then she, too, caught sight of the full beauty of those trout.

"Hell!" she breathed.

Chapter XVI

Maisie

*

I am not quite sure what I had been doing—
arranging about some pointing, I think, up at
Outershaw—but in any case it does not matter.
It was a fearfully hot day; one of those on which
my valley seems to be a veritable sun-trap, holding
the heat as in a prism. Towards eleven or so it had
become almost unbearable. I decided to walk home
by way of the river side, taking advantage of what
shade there might be beneath the trees.

I have told you somewhere before, I believe, that
Ridsdale had planted various shrubs and bushes
along one side of the little lawn which slopes up
from the pool at Foggyshaw. I was walking along
on the outside of this row of bushes—now grown
into a flowered hedge of, in most places, more than
man height—when I happened to glance, quite
casually, across one of the lower places towards the
river. I gasped in sheer amazement. I thought my

eyes must be playing tricks with me, as they had done up at Icy Pool. For there, not twenty yards away across the strip of sunkissed grass, standing on a bare flat table of rock overhanging the water, was the nude figure of a girl. Her back was towards me; odd bits of lingerie lay round her feet; and, even as I looked, she stepped clear of the last of them. For a moment she paused at the edge of the rock; her arms outstretched; the golden sunlight playing full upon her. Then, like a flash, she was gone.

It was a very polished dive. The slim body seemed to shoot through the air and into the water like an eel.

I do not think I had quite gathered my wits together when I happened to catch sight of George hurrying along the path towards me. "Well," thought I, in a pretty twitter of excitement; "whatever else it may be, this is no place for George." Luckily he was still some distance away. I hurried on to stop him.

"There's a gentleman to see you, sir," he exclaimed. "Mary sent me to find you, but I've forgotten what name she said. A plump, jolly-looking gentleman, with a sunburned face and horn-rimmed glasses."

Well, the only person I could think of to fit that description was the Aga Khan. I could not tell who it might be. We turned back together and went up to the house to see.

I recognized him fifty yards away. In all the world there could be but one good-natured shape like that. I almost whooped in my excitement. "Tom Gahan," I yelled, "Tommy, Tommy, Tommy." I ran towards him, both hands outstretched. Big Tom Gahan, from Chicago . . . grinning.

"What the hell!" I cried. "What the. . . ."

The last time I had seen Tom Gahan was in Chicago eight years before. He had shown me round, a stranger, and extended to me hospitality of a charm and lavishness which I could never in my life forget. Older than I was, by a dozen years or more, he had taken me under his wing and given me a royal time. A great big house he lived in, I remember, installed with all manner of fantastic gadgets which he had invented, so he said, to save labour. They amused me vastly, these *lares et penates* of his. It took longer to put one into work than to do the job itself. That is at least with some of them; others went off with the suddenness of a Mills bomb. Mrs. Gahan was dead, but there had been a youngster, I recalled; a long-legged, towheaded, altogether delightful slip of a girl about ten or twelve years old called Maisie.

We pump-handled each other out there on the lawn for a full five minutes; dancing round each other like a couple of Pawnee Indians gone cuckoo.

"Let's go inside and have a drink," I gurgled, when at last I had enough breath gathered to speak at all, "and tell me all about it. Oh, Tommy; you of all people. How long can you stay? How did you get wind of my being up here? How . . . ?" I must have asked a score of questions.

He passed his great arm round my shoulders and very gently, but very firmly—Gahan had superb strength—turned me towards the cool interior beyond my open door. "Where's that drink, buddy?" he inquired, softly.

I led him to it.

We sat there perhaps half an hour, asking each other questions; some of which we answered, and some of which we overlooked in our eagerness to ask others. I mentioned a score of friends. "And Maisie?" I inquired.

Gahan suddenly stopped and stared at me. "Gee," he said, "Maisie's somewhere around. I'd forgotten her. She was going to give your garden the once-over and then come back. I guess she's wandered afield. We'd better get off after her, maybe, eh?"

I thought not. "She'll be all right," I said.

"Quite a big girl now I suppose, Maisie?"

Gahan grinned. "You won't know her," he said, proudly. "Nineteen now; twenty almost. N'York —London—Paris—she's tried them all; and"—he clapped me upon the knee—"the best place of all, she tells me, is that old ranch of mine you saw down at El Paso. Spent all last year there, running loose liked a young colt."

There was no disguising old Tom Gahan's delight at this fact. He was one of the "wide-open-spaces" brigade, and he loved his daughter to be so too. We babbled for another half hour; mostly Maisie.

"But look here," he concluded, rising. "That girl's somewhere around. Let's go look."

We had not to go far. As we stepped out into the garden we saw her coming across the grass towards us; a tall, slender, bare-headed girl with hazel eyes which turned golden when she smiled. Her pale-coloured hair, still wet, shone and glistened in the sun. She remembered me, she said; but I think it must have been but a hazy memory. I myself would not have known her; though now, as she stood there before me, I caught myself remembering and re-recognizing little mannerisms both of speech and gesture. They had been attractive then: now they were enchanting. In fact she was enchanting altogether. Old Tom Gahan had been right. Maisie nowadays was something very specially delightful; very specially delightful indeed.

We spent the afternoon among my roses. I had never spent so long a time before in a garden. Somehow I had always seemed to wander on and on until I was out of it, trying to find a beck or something. I think Pan must have been lying in wait for me when I was born. But now the ordered loveliness of that garden fell full upon me. The soft, quiet lawns and trees; the flaunting livery of the flowers; the exquisite peace and calmness which seemed everywhere—I was very happy, that one day, just to laze away the sunlit hours in such surroundings.

And with such friends.

It was well after tea before the call of the blood showed itself in Tom. I had told him of my river and all that I had done to make it good. He had been interested; for Tom himself held a lease on some strangely named stream up in Canada. He had got as far as saying that he "must see it some time"—but that is as far as he *had* got.

Now in the quiet of the evening; with the crescent moon, a thread of beauty, hung in the southern sky; we strolled between the banks of honeysuckle down to the packhorse bridge. I had made the view from there particularly attractive. My little stream, under the soft lights of the setting sun, looked exquisite. Save where the dark shadows of the trees were touching them, the pools mirrored the sky; the runs between them laughed and gurgled over the brown stones. Blooms Ridsdale had planted glowed here and there like jewels; gazing, like Narcissus, into the water; more than half-aswoon, it seemed, with their own loveliness. The soft crying of the plovers, calling still for Deirdre, came unceasingly from the pastures among the hills; hills clothed themselves in sheerest magic. And over everything there stole the lingering fragrance of a million flowers.

Maisie's hand sought mine where it lay upon the old stone breastwork of the bridge; covered it a moment and was then withdrawn. I dared not look at her.

"And you tell me there are trout in there?" broke in Tom, the vandal.

"Lashings," I lied glibly. "Big ones."

"I'll bring a rod and some new plug-baits I've got. I'll cable for 'em. Maise, we are coming to stay here." He turned to me. "Next week, huh?"

"Before," I suggested. "Why not . . .?"

"Must have a rod," he interrupted, "and I like my own. Anyway I have some things to do, and

Maisie's got some friends to see. Isn't that so, Maise?"

She nodded absently, her eyes still far away.

"But," he continued, turning once more to me, "about the end of next week, eh?"

"Yes, of course," I cried. "Whenever you can. . . ."

We turned back towards home. Tom looked at his watch; started as he caught sight of the time; and sent Maisie on ahead for the car. It was outside the gates as we drew up. And there, coming along one of the paths was George; with, resting across his arm, the biggest bunch of roses I had ever seen. The choicest blooms, too. I could not have selected better ones myself; not as good, probably. He offered them to me; but I was not going to rob the old chap of his gallantry. I led him gently towards the lady in the car. Poor old George . . . it was his garden she had loved: his was the gift, not mine.

I did not hear what Maisie whispered; but I wished she had said it to me. Then George, cap in hand, backed away. "Tha mun come ageean, my lady," he invited her, with a sidelong look at me. "Tha mun come ageean, an' welcome."

Gahan got in, and I moved round the car. Maisie bent forward to her gears.

"Good-bye," said he, across her. "We'll be back next week."

"That's right," said I. "If we can't fish, we can bathe. There is a first-class pool just up the river, with a little lawn of its own, and a nice flat rock you can dive off, and a. . . ."

Maisie glanced at me quickly out of her eye-corners. I met her look squarely enough; but I am afraid my mouth quivered. There was a moment's startled pause, and then a wave of delightful colour surged up to the very roots of that glorious corn-coloured hair.

"Pig!" she laughed, and nearly ran over my foot.

Chapter XVII

Groins and Gypsies

*

L et us get back to my river. There have been too
   many interruptions. I will go back to the time
   when I made my lake.

For a week or two afterwards I was a bit scared
of groins. Their effect, like that of the genie of the
button, struck me as being "too wholesale". Still,
at the same time, I had a sneaking hankering after
more. There were many straightish little bits up
and down the stream which, I thought, would look
better if they were wriggled about somewhat: little
bays and underhangings made here; eddies there;
and so on. The only way this could be done, apart
from digging—and I had had enough of digging!
—was by throwing the main force of the water on
to one bank; then, a few yards below, on to the
other, and so creating a more broken stream than
the straight, fast current which was there already.

And the easiest method of doing this—as I knew

from experience—was by the building of groins out from the sides.

Still, I could not afford to have many spectacular successes like my last. I had to live upon rents, and the first thing I looked at, when I came to a straight bit, was the quality of the land on either side. I was having no lucrative meadows submerged. That one odd pasture did not matter; but it was enough.

I held an overweening respect for the force of these moorland spates now. I knew that the explanation of the excessive flooding lay in the fact that I had made my groin too large, too high and strong; and that probably a smaller one would behave as I expected it to do. But still; most of that bottom land was soft and rich. Thousands of gallons a minute, coming with the rush it did, would soon scoop out that sort of stuff. Rock there might be somewhere underneath which might check it—but where?

I walked up and down that river more than once in thoughtful mood. Wire-netting I thought of; and so I did, too, of the unsightly board dams, wondering how I could adapt them.

It was the gypsies who gave me my clue. I came across them one day quite suddenly. I was walking slowly down the stream, when from the distance ahead I caught the strains of someone singing. A sad little song it was, one that I did not know; and sung in a quiet, gentle voice as though done almost unconsciously. I walked on towards it, round a couple of bends; and there I saw the owner of the song. She was a young girl, twelve or thirteen I should say, with the dark eyes and olive skin these people wear so well. A wee sprawling baby lay at her feet, almost naked, and with fat, chubby limbs kicking happily into the air. The singing stopped suddenly as I hove into view; the girl looking at me levelly as I approached. She made no attempt to rise—at which I was glad. By her side was a little heap of strong willow shoots, freshly cut, from which she was trimming off the leaves, then tying into bundles.

Without further ado, I squatted down beside this Arcadian couple, and in two minutes we were friends. The youngster was chuckling more merrily than ever as my fingers poked among his ribs; and the girl, her shyness overcome, was chattering away to me as though she had known me all her life. I had heard and read of the reserve of these folk, but I found none here. The willow shoots, she told me, were for sheep hurdles which they sold to the farmers, and the finer ones they wove up into baskets.

"And where", I asked, "is the caravan?" I supposed there was a caravan somewhere.

She turned and pointed over towards the lane running across the valley. "Over there," she explained. "Look, you can see the smoke."

I looked. A thin wisp of smoke was rising through the trees flanking the road, and I remembered that there was a little patch of grassland at that particular corner of the road. I picked up the youngster and placed him on my shoulder. "Come along," I said. "Let us go and see if tea is ready."

She laughed at that, but gathered up her bundles and fell in beside me.

The little camp was where I thought it was. A caravan lay drawn up on the grass, and a tethered horse nibbled quietly at the less dusty herbage in the hedge bottom. A tiny fire had been lighted, from which a thin column of pale blue, scented smoke rose straight up towards the sky. By its side, seated on a fallen log, was an old crone, staring into the embers and puffing stolidly at a dark clay pipe. A youngish man, with one whom I took to be his wife, were busy plaiting hurdles as they sat. Both rose as we approached; the woman gazing fearfully at the burden I so lightly carried. She smiled in obvious relief as I hauled him down from his precarious perch and, with a final tickle, handed him across.

I seemed to have broken down that fabled reserve

here as well, for the man greeted me civilly enough; his white teeth showing in a delightfully open smile as I drew out my tobacco and sat down on a log opposite the old woman. The little girl was standing shyly at my side. I drew her on to one knee and made myself at home.

A lithe, likeable fellow was that lad. He would not be more than twenty-two or three; slim and cleanly-built, and with his muscles hard as iron. I could see that. The elder girl—his wife, as I had presumed—was personable enough, too; though her shyness was more difficult to overcome. She stood at the foot of the steps leading down from the caravan, her baby on her arm, watching us as we talked.

"These farm hurdles," I began at last, the ordinary civilities being past; "I myself want some of them, but I want them more stoutly built—thicker branches, you understand. Can you do that?"

He nodded. "If we can get the withies, we can," he explained.

Well, there was no difficulty about that. I knew a dozen places in the valley where they could be found. I said so. Again he nodded, and I told him, in explanation, what they were for. "I want to make groins," I explained, "running out into the river there, so that I can turn the water where I want it. I think I shall need at least a hundred."

"Yes," he said, "we can make a hundred. You will want the stakes long, so that you can drive them well in. How long?"

It was a point I had overlooked for the moment. I made a rapid calculation. "Four feet," I said; "and very strong."

We left it at that. "Let me know when you have the first dozen ready," I told him. "I live up there." I pointed up towards where my house lay hidden among the trees.

I think he knew that already, for he asked for no further directions; just nodded soberly and rose as I did. The little girl slid off my knee and went beside him. His arm rested round her shoulders. A sudden thought struck me. I was detaining these people in my valley longer than, perhaps, they had intended to stay. There was a question of supplies. "I will pay for the first lot now," I said, drawing out a note; "and the others. . . ."

But he would have none of that. "No," he replied. "When we have finished, and you are satisfied."

I liked this young chap immensely. There was no sign here, that I could see, of that traditional, eastern-like autocracy in the treatment of his women folk. His regard for them was obvious. His wife came forward now, all smiles, and leant her arm upon his shoulder, looking at me appraisingly. The baby had apparently been put to bed.

A sudden croak came from the old body seated by the fire. "Read the gentleman his hand, Liz," she chuckled, "before he goes."

"No, no," laughed her son—for this I later found him to be—"we don't. . . ."

But my hand was already extended. I waved his protestations aside. "Several journeys across the water," I laughed, "making groins. What else?"

The slim brown fingers took the tips of mine. I missed the first few things, I am afraid, in wondering at the surprising quality of that hand; but I caught the "dark woman" business crossing my path. At that there was an interruption. A hoarse cackle came from the log by the fire. "Dark?" scoffed the old body; "dark? No; *fair*! Fair do I see her; fair as the ripening wheat. Tall she is, and hazel-eyed, among the flowers."

I slipped the young kiddie half a crown. How that old hag knew, I cannot say. She had never even looked at me. But she was too damn near right for my liking. I went home before she told me something else.

However, my groins were arranged for, and in time they were made. I brought a maul down with me one afternoon, and the gypsy lad and I put the first lot in. I liked them. They threw the water just hard enough to eat out a little of the opposite bank. They were green at present. I had hopes that some of the shoots might strike down into the gravel beds eventually and grow.

No fear of these doing damage, I thought. I put them in sloping gently downstream; and I took pains to see that they did not divert too great a press of water. The thought of floods held me in thrall. But *these* groins should be all right, I concluded. They were not high enough to stop a real spate in any case. In a heavy flood the extra water would go over the top. And they did not reach far enough across to scoop out the other side unduly, whatever happened.

We got them all in during one dry spell, and I settled up with my Romany friends. I was genuinely sorry when they went. I watched their little cavalcade go winding up the hill road to the north; halt for a moment at the top; and then pass slowly out of sight across the crest.

The first freshet which came down altered the whole aspect of these long, straight stretches. Sand and gravel piled up against the groins on the up-stream side; holes and hollows were scooped out of the opposing banks; and—what pleased me most, I think—behind every groin, between it and the bank on the downstream side, a fairly deep eddy formed, with its centre—the deepest part—just off the end of the groin and its bottom shelving up towards the bank. A really attractive bit of water; and, I am sure, a very welcome shelter to the trout in times of flood. They could lie snug behind the cover of those groins.

And no mere theory this, either! I had not long to wait for proof. After every freshet one could see them gathered there—if the water were not too darkly coloured—a dozen of them, perhaps; lying in that quiet, gentle water, with the stream itself tearing madly past a yard or so away.

I laid down those groins in series, too: three or four at a time behind each other at intervals of perhaps ten or a dozen yards. I remembered my lesson of the dams. The top groin would silt up level, I knew; but those others would keep fairly clear.

And, in time, many of those willows struck. I let them grow. They broke up every semblance of artificiality; and I dare say paid their full quota to the commissariat. They were favourite spots for trout, those quick eddies. One could get a fish there almost any time; even when every other place was "dead". Good, trouty water, all of it. I often think my debt to those quiet gypsy folk is still one half unpaid.

Chapter XVIII

Possessed of Devils

*

There remained but little now to do; save perhaps to improve some of the tributary burns. Field drains and such small waters I had altered beyond all knowing. Instead of being half-hidden ditches, blocked with stones and clods of earth, they were now rippling, little, gravelly-bottomed streamlets in themselves. Some I had widened; some built up. In most I had planted cress and marigolds. Every little gutter or trickle I had come across I had speculated upon what use I could make of it; and, where practical, had put my ideas into being. I had added miles and miles of good, food-bearing water to my river.

And now, as I say, there were but few places where any further work was needed. The Keld Water occupied most of my time, I think. There, if you remember, the stream comes pitching down from the hills in steep cascades and waterfalls, and then runs, comparatively quietly, for its last few hundred yards. It is a place I have always had in mind as a little backwater in which to maroon some guest whom it were better to have by himself.

There are such people, you know. Sober folks who take their fishing ultra-seriously, and see no lighter side to it at all. I once had two of them together; men who had lived long in India. They cursed fish by day and talked "pig" all night.

It was for such as these that I wanted the Keld Water. I would keep their minds occupied. It was good water to begin with, and there was a big head of trout in the lower reaches. The higher-lying pools I had finally decided to leave alone. They were totally unmanageable. The rapid fall of the stream made the thoughts of any dams impossible —to get twenty yards of flat water would have meant a wall ten or twelve feet high. I concentrated on improving the size of the fish inhabiting it. This I did in the same way that I had done all those others. I planted beds of cress and marigolds in every possible situation. I threw boulder groins across—they could do no harm up here—to twist the stream a little; and I made use, wherever it was possible at all, of low wire-netting weirs to keep the gravel-beds submerged.

But it was the bottom length I specialized in

most. Here was water of a delightful nature to begin with. Its one fault lay, perhaps, in the fact that it was too easy. I set out to alter that. I wanted my "maroons" to be kept busy. There were many pools; dark, lovely pools; where a minnow, I knew, would be absolutely deadly. And a minnow would be used too, I knew, by some of the gentry I had in mind, once they found that flies were rather "off".

Well, a few snags and tree roots would alter that. I cut willow shoots and planted them. I dug up thorn bushes, complete, and heaved them in; staking them down fast as best I could. Odd stumps and rocks I used as often as I found them; and at the spots where it was really difficult to cast owing to overhanging trees; there, by means of dams and such-like devices, I tried to make the most likely holds for trout.

One place pleased me particularly. The stream ran deep down between high banks all garrisoned with gorse and brambles and wild roses. It formed a wind-tunnel whenever there was any breeze at all: a difficult, unchancy place to cast; for the footing, too, was bad at any time. I made the footing worse and the water better. I made it the best-looking length on the stream. I made it irresistible. Whatever happened, I knew that the type of man I would maroon here could never leave that bit unfished.

He would not be able to. Its challenge simply could not stay unanswered.

As a solace I planted gooseberry and raspberry bushes where they were needed. I thought that while they were untangling their caught-up casts, they could—if it should be the proper season—at least console themselves by nibbling at the fruit. For a time I toyed with the idea of hemlock. After the third or fourth cast, perhaps . . . if the wind were really bad. . . .

But I have felt like that myself . . . too often.

I put in some very thorough work at that spot. A fish had no need to wander far before he had the angler's mind somewhat unhinged. Wherever there was a chance to make a difficulty, either in the water or above it, I made it. All the time I had in mind just one particular type of man. You will know him as well as I do. The one who is so damnably efficient that one hates him instinctively. I knew one such; once indeed he had been up to see me. He had smiled, in his condescending way, at my enthusiasms; had crabbed my dams, my rods, my flies, my fish—my everything. He had been superior to every last thing that I had. "I will *send* you some flies," he had said. But he must have forgotten, for I never got them. Which was just as well: they would have gone on the fire anyway.

Possessed of Devils

Well, I made the Keld Water for such as he. You can imagine what it was like. I think I must have been possessed of devils. But the fish were there; good fish; the best that I had. *They* were the bait!

The Woogill water I also altered for, I think, the better. It is a dubious point this, for that stream had always held some subtle appeal all its own. I had been careful, all through, to keep the character of my streams unimpaired. All I had done was to accentuate the more attractive features and hide up the less. This had been easy in most places.

But Woogill was different. At some time or other there had been a terrific cloudburst up at its head. The sudden mass of water had torn and riven its banks into a tumbled ruin of broken earth and rock. It must have been a wild scene of desolation as the waters abated, but now the sides were clothed once more with vegetation; there remained but the widened stream-bed with its huge, up-jutting rocks and piled-up boulders. Dams had been formed naturally. Wherever there was a bend in the stream, there was a high-massed heap of stone; under every fall there had been scoured out a deep-cut hole. Eddies had formed; ever-circling pools of dark brown, foam-flecked water. There were quick, fast runs and falls—falls galore; drops of anything from

223

a few inches to half a dozen feet. It was difficult to know where to begin.

I decided to start from the bottom and work up as far as seemed practicable. Then I would leave it in its natural state—attractive enough for any normal being as it was. I could imagine nothing much more delightful in its way than fishing up that stream with say an odd partridge-hackled fly and casting on to those eddied pools and runlets. It would be neat, accurate work; by no means finished when the trout was "on". They cropped up every yard or two it seemed, these holes; sometimes two alongside each other. Difficult water to alter; very difficult.

Still I could do something. There were plenty of sand and gravel beds to cover, and so improve the hatch of fly. That I could do, at any rate. Since Ridsdale's lectures I detested seeing such ground wasted. Well, there was stone handy enough. To make a dam at any place would not necessitate rolling a boulder above a couple of feet.

I set to work.

In no time, it appeared, I had a score of dams thrown haphazardly across. One single block of stone moved into a gap was often sufficient (save for the smaller pebbles and sand I shovelled up against it) and soon the rougher features of the stream had almost disappeared. The bigger rocks, of course, still stuck out above the water, but I liked those. All the smaller ones were covered; just gleaming brightly underneath the surface. At places I threw out groins; twisting the current a little so that one had to study hard at every pool one came across. One could never fish more than one or two in quite the same way. "Bogey three," I thought. It would take three casts to cover that hole properly; what with curling runs, and boulders, and over-hanging trees. I calculated, as I looked at it, that I myself would do well if I managed it in six.

Yes; Woogill I made into a delightfully tricky length of water. I went on and on—for it was easy work—making little pools where there were none before; enlarging those already there; splitting up too rapid runs; turning the current so that it ran towards one side rather than straight down the middle. I expended a good deal of ingenuity upon that particular stream. I followed it all the way up, almost on to the moor; and wherever there was a marshy spot, or a little quiet runlet coming in, there I planted marigolds or cress. I opened up a dozen stagnant bits of ponds I found in a dip, running a channel from them to the stream. If any tadpoles were hatched there, which I suspected there would be, well a percentage of them at any rate would find their way towards my trout. It was surprising the number of tiny feeders—mere trickles carrying no more water than a household tap—that I came across and made full use of. Little dams I formed, even on these. A stone or two just thrown across a narrow place was sufficient. It made an obstruction and the water backed up behind it, covering a foot-wide, yard-long bit of sand or gravel which was bare before. All fly-breeding places. They mounted up in the aggregate. I wasted nothing on Woogill.

Chapter XIX

How I made a Hatchery

*

The time had come to make a hatchery. I had so improved the food-bearing capabilities of my river that I was sure it could now carry a much greater head of trout than it actually possessed. In Burngill the fish were running up to spawn. I could see them congregating in all the little pools; sometimes a dozen of them in a space a few yards square; dashing about in wild excitement as I appeared on the bank. Other tributaries too, I found, held a vastly increased number of fish, all working their way up to the headwaters. They would spawn all right, I knew; but then I also knew what would happen should a storm come. I could see it all: the gradual gathering of the waters; the fresh little runnels starting, growing, and then streaming into the becks. And the becks growing; turning into wild, dark, foaming torrents pouring headlong down the ghylls. Whole gravel-beds would be washed away. I thought of all my dear little ova being trundled over miles and miles of river-bed; bumped across weirs; and carried out to sea. It was horrible.

And there were other enemies, too. Herons, wild duck—oh, a host of troubles. Why, the trout themselves ... they were not above a spot of cannibalism either, I believed. I must make a hatchery—at once.

Luckily I was well placed. There was no end to the number of little streams where I could depend upon a constant flow. The amount of water coming down needed to be regulated; that was all. In fact there were a dozen places close to the house.

I set off to select one.

My mind was full of breeding trout now. All my gardening and dams and weirs were clean forgotten. I lived for the sake of saving ova. "Restocking" —that was my fetish. The wee, tiny streams running out of old cattle troughs; I stopped at all of them, following them down as they trickled, gin-clear and sparkling, over their tiny gravel-beds. They laughed and gurgled with a new note to me, like stranger children whom one found delightful. I fell in love with all of them; examining each individually and with unexpected fascination. I would come across a little yard-wide pool, with golden water rippling, a few inches deep, over jewelled gravel the size of peas. Shade there would be from the overhanging tufts of meadowsweet; and food, I knew, washed down from the marshy places of the stream. "What a little heaven for an alevin!" laughed I.

But still; when the first wild enthusiasms had worked off, I realized that this restocking was a serious business. I knew nothing much about it, really; save what I had picked up from a few odd papers. I wondered if there were any books on the subject. Ridsdale would know. I put through a hurry-call to him by wire.

I hung about all day, waiting a reply, but nothing came. Nor did the post bring anything the next morning. I cursed him very fluently. This was not the treatment I expected from a co-partner.

I was mooning round the garden, still muttering away to myself, when a rather spectacular two-seater car came whizzing through the gates and roared up the drive. Two sleek young men with horn-rimmed glasses and no hats descended. "What the devil are *they* selling?" I growled impatiently, my mood being still upon me.

One of the long-legged youths stalked towards me, smiling. I must confess that, as he drew nearer, I liked the look of him. His grin was infectious. I took the hand he held out towards me. "The governor sent us up," he explained. "Said you'd gone all broody and wanted to sit some trout eggs."

"The gov'nor?" I questioned, puzzled.

"My name's Ridsdale," he smiled.

"What—his son?" I cried, reaching for his hand again.

"Both of us," he replied. "I'm Chris. That misspent youth there by the car is Alec. He's come up to help me hold it down."

"Hold what down—the fish?"

He waved the suggestion aside with mock impatience. "No, no," he said; "that ale Mrs. Arnison brews. The old man. . . ."

"Look here," I interrupted, firmly. "What else did your father say? About a trout-hatchery, I mean. I expected a letter."

"He sent us instead."

I turned to see him smiling at me. I liked that smile. "Whatever for?" I asked.

"Well, of course, by the way he talked, we thought the main reason he sent us up for was to sample that ale"—he looked at me speculatively —"but"—his voice trailed off—"if you really want a hand with that hatchery. . . ."

"I do," I stated, definitely. "Know anything about them?"

He nodded towards the lad just leaving the car and coming towards us. "Alec does," he said.

They might have been twins. I had admired Ridsdale for all that he had done; but his best work was here, obviously. Alec was as charming as his brother.

"Come along inside," I suggested, taking an arm of each. "The bar's open; let's see if we can't find a substitute for this ale you tell me about."

"Quite a sound idea," commented Alec. "We left at six, and. . . ."

"You *what*?" I cried.

"Left at six. Wanted to get here early. We've got to be back tonight, you know."

"But," I said, "I thought you were going to help me with my hatchery?"

"Help you? We're going to *make* it! You only want a few thousand, don't you?"

I stared at this confident youth, with his casual "few thousand". But it was a genuine question. "I've three miles of decent water," I commented, "and a good deal of beck. I want to keep the stock up to its limit."

"We'll manage that all right. The pater said your fish were running now. We'll slip down and have a look at 'em." He refilled his tankard and drained it off again, it seemed without taking breath. "Should we go now?" he suggested, rising.

He was a quick mover, that boy. We seemed to

be down at Burngill in about five strides. He had a fish out, examining it, almost before I had drawn up at the bank. "Ripe," he commented.

"Do you know what I'd do here?" he asked, moving off up the stream. "I'd block the mouth of the beck so that no more fish could get up, and then cover the spawning redds with wire-netting. It's an excellent bottom. Constant flow, I suppose? Is it subject to flooding?"

"No," I said; "not much. It's so short, you see."

"Any watercress beds planted out?"

"Yes," I told him; "the stream runs through three or four big beds, and one of marigolds, too."

"Well, then, I'd leave this one if I were you. There are plenty of trout living in sin here already. Just cover over the spawning beds as much as you can with netting. Take out the gate at the bottom when you see the other fish in the main river have stopped running. Give 'em a week or two longer, anyway; they're all right up here. You'll be able to see when the spawned fish start dropping down; open your gate then."

Well, that was easy enough. "But I thought you wanted ponds and things—ponds for yearlings, two-year-olds, and so on?" I remarked.

"Not you!" he scoffed; "not up here. Stock with fry—it's the best way; far the best way. You don't want a lot of pampered parasites in the river who'll expect you to feed 'em by hand. Fry is the best. We'll make a hatchery for fry: that's all you—or anybody else—can want. Look after them up to May, say; and then dibble them in along the shallows and the sides of your pools. Put them in a watering-can and dibble them in. Spread them out well, in sensible places; that's all that you need do. Put them in round the mouths of your side streams —into the streams as well—spread 'em out." He looked at me seriously. "Spread 'em out," he repeated. "It's important."

"Fry cannot travel far to find food, you know," he went on. "They stop pretty well where they are put for some time. If they are dumped in in quantities you'll only attract enemies and lose them all. Spread 'em out. Put them down in every stream you've got."

He rather took my breath away, this Alec. All the time he talked, he was striding along with that great lope of his. I showed him half a dozen streams —all, it seemed fairly well-stocked with spawning fish.

"Now I'll tell you what to do," he said at last, turning me once more towards home. "On the streams where you don't anticipate severe flooding, or, as you say, you can pipe"—I had timidly mentioned piping to control a flow—"just cover over the redds as I suggest with wire-netting and leave them. The more watercress you have the better: the fry will drop down towards it and, you see, they'll *thrive*. You'll get a good crop."

"But, my hatchery?" I quavered. "I want a hatchery."

"Sure you do. We're going to make it now. Where would you like it? I'd have it somewhere near the house, if I were you. It'll be handier."

"I've got the very place. I looked it out some days ago."

"Right; let's go."

He was stalking along again as hard as ever. We caught up with him, standing gazing at a clear little stream which ran gently down opposite the end of my garden and flowed into Foggyshaw Beck. "What's the matter with this?" he inquired, looking up and down the length he could see.

"That's the one," I asserted, feeling bucked.

"Steady flow? No floods?"

"None," I assured him, quite truthfully. "It's an old overflow arrangement from the house reservoir," I explained. "We don't use it now, but it's piped higher up and all the flood-water goes straight down the beck; it can't get into here."

"Not spring-water, then?" he asked.

How I made a Hatchery

I shook my head. "Not this," I said.

"Good!" he commented. "Very good indeed. We can make a rattling good pond of it. What about food?"

"Cress almost all the way up," I said; "off and on. There are a couple of hundred yards of it, starting round the corner, and more below. Bar this bit, I think it is full of cress."

He smacked me across the back. "That's really excellent," he said. "Get the hatchery, Chris."

Chris laughed. "Right," he grinned.

He strode across to the car, and opening the dickey, he lugged out one of those abominable tin trunks which one sees occasionally, even yet, on railway platforms. It had seen good service, too, by the look of it. Though it seemed a rather quaint receptacle, I expected it to be full of those glass grille things I had read about. The way Chris pitched it out on to the ground, however, while he fastened the flap of the dickey, completely disillusioned me on that score. He came along, swinging it by one handle. Why, the thing was empty!

"What the devil's this?" I asked.

Alec looked at me quite soberly. "Why, that's your hatchery-box," said he.

"But . . . but . . . shouldn't there be fittings and things?"

"Not a bit. This is all we want. Get a chisel."

I thought I could detect Ridsdale Senior's hand in this. He had played on my innocence and sold me a pup. That old tin box had been a lively effort when it was new. Now it looked like a Nellie Wallace sort of joke.

"What do you want a chisel for?" I asked. "You'll spoil it."

He smiled faintly at that. "Get a chisel," he repeated, turning me towards the shed; "and a hammer. We're busy."

I got him the hammer and chisel, and in half a minute he had thrown back the lid and was punching holes everywhere he could in the sides and bottom of that horrible outrage of a box. It looked the most dissolute affair imaginable when he had finished; something remotely suggestive of a cross between a watchman's brazier, with the fire out, and a slum clearance.

"That's it," he commented, standing back and regarding his handiwork complacently. "That will do fine." He absently handed me back the hammer and chisel to get rid of. "Come along, we'll put it down."

He stalked off and selected a place to put it. "In here," he commanded. We lowered the frightful-looking thing into the water—it reminded me horribly of a burial—resting it on a couple of little stone supports that he had rigged up. We wedged it firmly into place, jamming it with bits of rock forced down between it and the banks.

"Now we want some gravel," he remarked, looking round. "Nice, well-washed gravel. Get a sieve, Chris; there's a big one hanging up in the shed." Ridsdale's observation powers had apparently been handed down: *I* didn't know there was a sieve there. However, Chris was back with it almost at once. We filled it with gravel from the beck; fine clean gravel the size of little peas; and thoroughly scoured it. We coated the floor of the box. Then we scoured a further lot—specially selected stuff which was subjected to a careful scrutiny and the bigger pieces picked out before it was passed. This lot we left in the sieve, ready.

"Now," said he; "a couple of buckets apiece, and a soup plate or two. . . ." He turned to me, interrogatively.

"Right," I said, "I'll get them." I led the way back to the toolshed again and told them to select what buckets they required while I went on to the house for the plates. I brought half a dozen.

Alec glanced at them. "Those will do A.1.," he said. "Put them down. We might as well do the job here; it's only a few yards away."

How I made a Hatchery

"Do any fish run up *this* stream?" he asked, as we left the shed with our buckets and reached the banks of Foggyshaw Beck.

"Not quite so far as this. There's a fall. Plenty at the bottom end, though—say fifty yards down."

"Good, big fish?"

"Yes, quite. Well, that is for up here, you know!" I hastened to add this in explanation. I did not want this god-like youth to be under any illusions.

"That will do then." We were off down the beckside before he had finished speaking.

He stopped at one of the little pools on the stream. It seemed to be full of fish. I could see the tails of half a dozen sticking out of the crowded shelter of a rock on the far side. There were others lying by the sides of stones in midstream. "We'll have that one," he said, pointing to a big one lying half under the rock, "and that one . . . and that . . . and that." He selected his fish without hesitation.

"Perhaps!" I thought to myself.

But he had half-filled a bucket and was laid down flat on the bank, with his sleeves rolled up, before I had time to think properly. In a couple of seconds he had his first fish lifted quietly out and lying still, curled round in the water at the bottom of the pail. Two or three others followed—selected fish—and then he called for another bucket. We got a dozen fish out of that pool and then moved on to another. Here, too, he chose his victims and caught them where they lay. It was uncanny. They seemed perfectly quiescent with him, and he lifted them out without any of the clutching I myself would have doubtless found to be necessary. We took over a score of trout back with us to the toolshed.

Once there, he sorted them: the five or six males in one lot; the rest—females—in another. Two or three spare buckets lying handy he also got Chris and me to fill and put down by his side. "For spent fish," he explained.

The proceedings were becoming exciting. He got hold of the half dozen big soup plates I had brought and spun them into line along the bench in front of him. His coat was already off and his sleeves rolled up. Now he fastened one of George's aprons in front of him. One sensed that tense feeling. The preliminaries were over. Something was going to happen.

His hand and arm dived down into that icy water. He brought out, quite gently and quietly, a female fish. He held her close over one of the plates; bending her back slightly as he did so. Immediately a stream of round, pinkish-coloured eggs, the size of little peas, flowed from her vent on to the plate. Then, holding her in his left hand, with the finger and thumb of the other—one each side of her body—he made a quick stroke down towards the tail. The last of the eggs were ejected. The fish was "stripped". He dropped her quietly into one of the spare buckets by his side.

Another female, and another, followed in quick succession. Two plates were full of eggs. A big, kip-jawed male—a really tough-looking brute—was taken up next. His milt, extracted in the same way, was directed over the mass of ova. Then he, too, was put on one side.

Both plates were now taken up and gently shaken until the milt was spread completely over and through the level mass of eggs. Alec drew a couple of feathers from his vest pocket, handing one across to Chris. All doubtful places were softly stirred with these.

"Right?" he called. "Right," answered Chris. The two dishes were carried across the few yards to the hatchery box, and the mass of—I hoped—fertilized eggs spread carefully upon one corner of the gravel lying on its bottom. The water ran very gently over them, bright and clean.

Back again—they were very quick, these two—and another lot of fish was spawned and the eggs laid in the box.

We got to the last pair. "Care to try?" asked

How I made a Hatchery

Alec. I nodded eagerly. I had been itching to try for some time. At least it seemed some time; actually, I suppose, it was but a few minutes. I took off my coat, rolled up my sleeves, and donned the apron Alec passed across to me. "This one first," he pointed out; "this is the hen." I dived my hand in, as he had done. The shock of the cold water almost numbed me for a second. I think I handled her too roughly, though I tried not to; for a little stream of eggs spurted from her as I lifted. However I got her over the plate and ran my finger and thumb down her as I had watched him do. The eggs shot out on to the plate. It startled me to find what a tiny pressure was required. Then I dropped her among the others.

The male now!

I got him at the third attempt, and I spawned him, too; stirring the milt over the eggs in the way that I had been shown.

"Capital," commented Alec. "Put them down now."

I carried my plate across and spread my eggs over the remaining corner of the box. As I rose to my feet again, the water washed away the last cloudy traces of the milt. There were the eggs; spread levelly over the gravel. They looked fine. "How many?" I asked.

How I made a Hatchery

"Oh, maybe ten thousand," answered Alec. "Hold this sieve."

He very gently spread the fine gravel it contained over the eggs; perhaps an inch of it; levelly, very carefully. And at last he closed down the lid and straightened up.

"There now," he said, smiling at me. "There's your hatchery. Cover over everything with wire netting; all the pool. That is all there is to do. The eggs will hatch out and the alevins make their way out of the holes to forage for themselves."

He thought for a moment. "It's December 15th now, isn't it? December 15th? Well, they may be all right without any feeding. However we will see. You'll have a hefty lot of fry by May, when you want to put them in the river."

"Ten thousand!" I said, doubtfully; wondering where to put them. "They. . . ."

"You won't get ten thousand," he laughed; "or anything like it. They've a trick of disappearing, have fry. But you'll have enough for the time being —quite enough."

I looked down at that horrible thing lying there in the stream. How different to the shining glass grilles and elaborations I had planned.

I think he read my thoughts. "Not quite what you expected?" he smiled. "Thoughts running on grille-boxes and yearlings and two-year-olds?"

I grinned my confession.

"A hatchery of the sort you have in mind is a full-time job," he assured me, seriously. "It's no pastime for an amateur; either breeding or feeding. And you don't need it," he added. "That is where your watercress and marigold planting comes in. You'll get a vastly increased percentage of wild fry maturing as a result of that. Don't forget you have all those other fish spawning naturally in the streams. You will have a big stock in a year or two."

I began to brighten up.

"I suppose fry *is* the best?" I queried, dubiously.

"Plenty of argument there," he laughed. "You'll have to take my word for it—for a year or two. *I* think so. But put them in properly," he went on. "Don't dump them in any old how. Do as I told you—dibble them in, one or two at a time, on the shallows and along the edges of the pools and below where streams come in—and, of course, in the streams themselves. Put them down anywhere where it is clean water and there is food about. And put them in late enough—say the middle of May. That is one of the main things to remember about fry. They must not be put in until there is a sufficient natural supply of food for them. Will you remember that?"

How I made a Hatchery

Chris made a peculiar clucking noise in his throat. "Talking about remembering," he drawled, "what about Arnison's? Do you know it's after three o'clock and getting dark?" He turned to me, smilingly. "How far do you say it is to Outershaw?" he asked.

"Too far," I said. "But if one cannot go to the mountain. . . ." I looked at them, blandly. "There has been an eighteen-gallon cask of Outershaw ale waiting in my cellar for the last six months."

Chapter XX

And a Fly-Farm

*

I think it was by accident that my fly-farm was founded. I remember it was one August day when I was doing some repairs to one of my groins that the idea first entered my head. I wanted some sort of support to stand on, and I remembered that, quite close by, over one of the little side-streams running down through the fields, there used to be an old plank bridge thrown across from one side to the other. One of those boards would do.

It was only a few yards away, and I set off towards it. However when I got there I discovered that the structure had long since fallen into disrepair. Cattle had used it to cross from one pasturage to another and, as is the way of cattle, they had made a marshy quagmire of the approaches. The sides of the stream had fallen in, and the half dozen planks which had formed the bridge were lying, sodden, half in, half out of the water.

Still, one of them would serve my job. I started

to drag it out on to dry land. The thing, soaked as it was, was plaguey heavy; and in the process it happened to turn over. I noticed at the time, and with distaste, that what had been the underside was covered with a mass of wet, slimy stuff; but it was only when I started to scrape this off, preparatory to shouldering the plank, that I saw what it actually was; that its real significance burst upon me.

It was a mass of eggs; thousands and thousands and thousands of them. There were a dozen or more river flies crawling about among them; females, I supposed, on the job. I stared at them hard. Why, here was where the flies bred; millions by the look of things. Why had Ridsdale not mentioned these, when he was so full of covering up my gravel-beds? Then I remembered: he had mentioned stone-flies particularly—perhaps he had forgotten or overlooked these others. But here was fish food in embryo—fish food galore. I lugged out those other five planks. They were all the same; their submerged ends completely smothered with flies and eggs.

Luckily I had a pretty powerful lens with me. I generally carried one with me as a matter of course so that, if I wished, I could examine the gullets of any fish I caught. Through this I examined the planks in greater detail. The store of food sprang upon me more vividly than ever. Among the eggs,

And a Fly-Farm

I could also now make out, not tens or scores, but hundreds of newly hatched nymphs—hundreds and hundreds. I was astounded.

My groin went unrepaired. I was too full of this new discovery. I had catered for the needs of those other flies, the ones which bred on gravel beds; now I would attend to these. If they wanted boards to lay their eggs on, they should have them. In every likely place I would introduce boards. And why limit their nesting places to planks? I would make rafts and breed more!

I got on to George straight away. Between us we made forty or fifty good big platforms, coating them with bitumen to prevent rot. Then we carried them to the side streams. I let them float down until they struck a narrow place and anchored of themselves, wedged in between the banks. In the river itself, too, I put a few; choosing the quiet backwaters screened by bushes where they would not be unduly conspicuous. These few, of course, I fastened down, fixing them in likely places and, so far as I could, out of the way of possible floods.

But I knew those floods. I knew that if they made their minds up they would make short work of ephemeral eggs—or flyboards either, for that matter. Still, there they were, for good or ill. About those put down in the smaller streams I had no qualms. I chose the places and I chose the streams. Flooding would not seriously bother those.

It was on the Monday that we put the boards in. On the following Saturday I thought I would like to see how they were getting on. I very gently lifted one out from the quiet corner where I had put it. It was covered—literally covered. Eggs and flies; eggs and flies—thousands! Out came my lens again, but I could see no nymphs. Still, what did that matter? There would be soon.

Every two days I examined the board, but it was a fortnight before I saw results. Then the nymphs started showing. And I may say here that they kept on showing until towards the end of September or so. Fresh lots of eggs were laid, hatched out, and fresh ones laid again. It was a continuous process. But towards September I saw fewer and fewer nymphs. Eggs there were a-plenty; but they did not seem to be hatching. I thought they were dead. By the end of the next month I was sure. Those others had hatched out quickly—fourteen days. I removed my boards from the river.

Those laid in the side streams I did not bother about. They were in nobody's way and would take no harm. The same thing had happened there, for I examined quite a few of them and found the eggs on them, too, apparently lifeless.

And a Fly-Farm

I say "apparently" for it was not until about the end of the following March that I found out that these very eggs were actually hatching out. I had meant to have my boards down in good time—for it was yet full early for any great hatch of fly on these upland streams—and for this reason had gone round them again. The ones on the river I had re-floated; it was those odd boards which had been left down all winter on the side streams which told me the truth. The masses of eggs were still there, and looking surprisingly healthy. Out came my lens. Why, there were nymphs! The eggs were fertile; or some of them at least; were even now hatching into flies. They were *alive*!

Now I knew those were the same eggs. I had examined the clusters too carefully to be mistaken; and in any case, there had not been mature flies of that sort about as yet—to that I could swear. They were last Autumn's eggs, hatching out after a winter's sleep; the eggs from which the first of the new season's flies were born.

Funny; I had not thought of that! Those early flies must hatch out from something. What else could it be but last season's crop; those lifeless-looking eggs lying out all winter, waiting for spring?

Well, that was that. In future *all* my boards remained down permanently. I made more of these board rafts, anchoring them where I thought most suitable. And in the following summers I got my reward.

I will go back to the time of my first discovery: that of the planks.

I started looking for eggs after that. I found them everywhere—on the reeds; on the bankside grasses; under stones; everywhere. I grew intensely interested. My introduction to the alder fly was given me by the trout themselves. I was sitting by the stream-side, just by the edge of one of my pools, when I noticed, lazily, an odd trout feeding close to the opposite bank. He rose continually; but more often appeared to take something under the surface. I wondered a little at this; for, just there, it seemed dead water; the current, such as it was, ran down *my* side. He went on steadily feeding for quite a while; so long, in fact, that at last I rose and crossed the stream to see. It was obviously something dropping from the bunch of reeds immediately above him. I examined these carefully; and there, in neat, compact brown patches, adhering to them, were bunch after bunch of eggs. They were hatching out. The larvæ fell to the water, dived to the bottom— I could watch them now, for the trout had gone— and burrowed into the mud. Interesting? It was fas-

cinating to me. It was fish-food! I looked round for
other bunches.

Nor had I, in fact, far to look. There were scores
of those neat, orderly clusters on the surrounding
bushes and vegetation; and many—too many—of
them I noticed, with a certain surprise, were not
overhanging the water at all. That must be altered.
I cut all the reeds I could find bearing eggs and
carried them carefully to the bank-side. There I
fastened them as best I could among the overhanging bushes and other plants, so that whatever larvæ
hatched would have no difficulty in finding water.

So much for alders.

But it was the stone flies which gave me my
greatest thrills. Fat, juicy mouthfuls; stone flies—or
their creepers either! In the spring, when I had been
constructing my boulder dams, I had seen literally
thousands of their shed skins washed up into all the
corners and lying along the edges of the gravel-
beds. A little later I saw the stone flies themselves.
I found them everywhere; great, gravid females
straying loose over the land. Why it should be so,
I do not know; but I used to find those errant
females, thousands of them, all heavily laden with
big clusters of brown eggs, wandering about in
the most unlikely places; especially, for some
reason—possibly because they were the most

conspicuous—on the white limestone roads and walls.

In subsequent springs I gathered up these females, and I transplanted their eggs, in water, to the covered gravel-beds of my pools. I do not know how many eggs I saved in this way; very many thousands, I should say, for I worked for days. I had to do something. Those hen stone flies appeared to me to be the most irresponsible of their sex. They were like a lot of solemn old women who had got lost and didn't care. "It did not matter—somebody would find them and put them right again."

And that somebody was myself.

I found out that many different sorts of flies will drop their eggs when dipped in water. Grannom will; so will caddis. The grannom rather startled me at first: those big bunches of eggs were such an amazing green.

Of March Browns I had a great supply. And what is more, they were in the valley until June. Not the August Brown or some other of the summer metamorphoses; the real, honest, genuine March Brown. They might have been off the river itself for a month or more, but I could always find them somewhere up on the higher reaches of the becks. March Browns did well in my valley.

May Flies were the only aliens I ever had the wish

to try. I loved May Flies for themselves; and I never see one but I think of one day in the Belgian Ardennes when I stumbled across a lake—a lake almost as lovely as mine—which was alive with them. They were in clouds; clouds like those of midges one sees on still, soft nights in summer. It was the biggest hatch that I ever saw; and in that setting, the most beautiful.

But May Flies were not for me now. They do breed, as a matter of fact, farther down the dale; and I got some weed and mud from one of their haunts which I carefully introduced into the quietest of my streams; one that I had dammed up specially and which had gently silted up. It seemed a good place to me; with a soft bed of detritus and everything for which any nymph could wish. But it was not to be. I looked in vain for May Fly the next two springs. If they did hatch out I did not find them. Nor have I seen, or heard of any since. I think that *they*, at all events, are dead.

Chapter XXI

My Valley People

*

And now I come to my valley people. I have told you all I know about my river; now I will tell you of the folks who live by its side. Some already you have met. Matt Arnison you know; and young McLeod I have touched upon. There remain but half a dozen or so more.

On the gentler lower slopes which lie wide of Burngill, there is a rather wonderful old Tudor cottage. "Netherside", they call it. It is long and low and many-windowed, and whitewashed every year. Upon its walls there grows a multitude of creepers; roses and clematis and a little red-flowering thing whose name I cannot, for the moment, call to mind. A little, old widow lady lives there now, all by herself. Invariably she is neatly dressed in black, with just a touch of white at neck and wrists. And somehow, always when I have called upon her, I have found her in her garden with her arms full of flowers. Perhaps—I do not know—she feels that they replace the three sons she has held there; three great sons who now stalk the stranger places of the earth in their own way. I met all three of them once on leave: three great, big, lean-visaged men with lovely teeth. They seemed to fill the valley.

But now, once more, this sweet old lady lives alone. Often I walk up to her home, taking perchance a brace of trout or so—or in their season other things, for always she is first upon my list. And yet I think it is myself more than any gift which I may bring that she appreciates. For she gives me jobs to do; gardening jobs which if I had them to do for any other body in the world I should most heartily detest. But here I somehow do them smilingly. Water I fetch her, two pailfuls at a time, from a distant spring; for though I piped her cottage the first year I was back, she still insists upon fetching all her drinking water in this way. And for some reason she is right. There is a sparkle to this unpiped water, when it is in a glass, that I can never get, try as I may, from the water in the tap. Invariably it amuses her, this test of mine. I try it every time I go.

Quite often we dine together: delightful meals which I could wish would never end. Her mind dwells restfully upon more spacious days than ours; days in which it must have been an unalloyed delight to live. She must have been a lovely woman then, for she still is good to look upon, even though now her hair is white and her eyes perhaps a little paled with age. Those years ago she must have been radiant. Her wit transcends that of any woman I have ever known: never have I heard laughter so softly gay, so happy and infectious.

Of course I may be biassed. I am her slave. I do everything she says, unhesitatingly. I cannot help it. I love doing it.

Then there is old John Lister; one of the original rogues left from "The '45" I think. He is the oldest man in the valley, and one of the hardiest. Wet or fine, it seems immaterial to him. I have met him in all weathers, far over the moor, generally bawling imprecations against what sounds to be a rough-legged buzzard, but which eventually turns out to be a sheepdog. He has sons and men to do his work, but he himself—outside the house, at any rate—is certainly a very present "boss". For coat he wears a long plaid shawl; though that, I think, save for a wild Highland accent, is his only concession to the land of his forbears. Horses and sheep he knows from A to Z; no doubt of that; even to an uncanny,

Scotch second-sighty knowledge of the price that wool will fetch next clip.

And it is over the hills he goes every Sunday. Five miles over the rough hill road to the little chapel at the head of the next dale. He preaches there sometimes and, judging from what I have heard in his own farmyard, I should say he was a pretty powerful exhorter, too.

Meet Mr. McNeith.

McNeith, Lister's head man, is one of the queerest, most lovable little fellows I have ever met. In spite of his name there is nothing even remotely Scotch about him. He comes from Barnsley way, among the coalfields; though you would not think that, either, from the look of him. He looks more like a Papuan than anything, though his face and hair are red. It is wonderful hair. In the pub parlours down at Badgerley he makes what he calls his "spending-brass" by letting strangers lift him—he is very small—by his hair. It is a matter of prescribed ritual, always. He selects his victims with an intelligence bordering on the malignant; deftly brings the conversation round to hirsute matters (never very difficult with Mac about) and then, before they know what they are about, he has them standing on a couple of those little round-topped iron

My Valley People

tables, perhaps a yard apart. With appropriate flourishes he takes up his stance between them. Their fingers reach down and fasten among the flaming locks, and at a word from him, they lift. Mac soars upwards into the air, his face perhaps a little redder than usual, but otherwise completely at his ease. He jerks vigorously up and down a few times, almost pulling the men off the tables, just to show that there is plenty of spare power; and then he rolls his eyes upwards and asks to be let down. Time is up. He has won his bet: there is no need to give too long a show. He may be asked to do it half a dozen times again, perhaps in different pubs. It is all the same to Mac. He is known, and welcomed, in them all.

These two, and McLeod, are the only aliens—for even if their forbears *did* come down with "The '45" and settled there, they would still—two hundred years after—be looked upon as "strangers". And why not? My valley and its people are very, very old. The gaunt churchyard across the hills is full of hardly decipherable gravestones as well as some more recent. But the names, even on the oldest stones, are the same as we have now.

And they were old names then! In yet more ancient title deeds they still crop up. Nay, more. Once I saw an old record of a grant made at the

258

founding of one of the monasteries Henry the
Eighth destroyed. Even there was my valley mentioned, and one name only was down there that I
did not know.

But then this dale was old before the Normans
came. The pit-dwelling Britons used it first, perhaps; and then the Romans; and after them, the
Danes. There is proof and to spare of all their
settlements. Often I pause upon my wanderings,
looking down upon the whole dear stretch of it
from some point of vantage. Here perhaps, on this
same spot, some dark, all-conquering Roman
stood; wondering, even as I, at all its loveliness;
comparing it, it may be, with some little valley of
his own homeland. Or, later than he, some flaxen
Dane, come up here to look for sheep.

Which is what Kit Metcalfe is always doing when
I meet him in such spots. There is little of the Viking
in Kit—or the Roman either. He is typically English. There is no other land on earth which could
have produced him. He can take his place with
nobles or with navvies, for he is equally at home
with either. He is distinguished: there is an air
about him somehow; a perfectly natural air which
draws and holds attention wherever he may be.
Only once or twice have I seen his counterpart—at
bloodstock sales many years ago. The clothes he

wears are invariably "right", and yet they are of a cut and pattern that not one man in a hundred thousand could ever hope to carry. It is his big extravagance, for they cost him dear. Still; it is worth it. I myself would, if he had need to ask, pay all their cost. Willingly I would do so; for the sight of him does me good. Kit lives a century or so too late. He would have filled his niche to perfection in the days of Hawker, Osbaldestone and those other bucks of the time.

And drink? He would have drunk a dozen of them dead!

He has some money of his own, of course, apart from sheep; the remnants of what I should think in his forbears' time must have been quite a considerable fortune. He told me once that his great-grandfather had rather hit the high spots in the sporting line, and it was left to his son—Kit's grandfather—to pull things together a bit. There had been no chance of further extravagances since, not real extravagances of such size, and now the present scion was reaping the benefit of three generations' saving; and was really, as things go, quite comfortably off. Nor has he kith or kin to care about. Kit is a bachelor; though that is an old story. The money that he leaves will, I know, go to the children, who, all down the dale, simply adore him. That is, all save a living for the old body, stone-deaf, who, with her son, looks after him.

His house, as one would expect, is a soft and mellow history of sport. There are fowling-pieces on the dark, oak-panelled walls; flintlocks, wheel-locks—a dozen of them and more; fishing rods and reels—reels with their home-made twisted horse-hair lines still on them; paintings of horses, of favourite hounds, of game-cocks; trophies of the chase in many lands. Here and there one comes across a sterner relic; the sword carried by a Metcalfe in the Civil War; another one at Flodden; others from the later campaigns in Spain and Flanders. Down through the years they come, these Metcalfe swords; right up to one which saw more of war than all of them together. For here, at the end of the line, bright as those others, hangs Kit's own blade.

My little valley was a famous place for game-cocks, by the way. A century ago they had an international reputation. Even to catch one was a day's job, for the Metcalfe of that day allowed them to run wild. They slept in trees, and were only brought in a few days before they were required. Kit tells me, too, how even in his time they were used by poachers for taking pheasants. One of the cocks would be taken in a basket along some country lane running near a covert side, and a keen lookout kept for a feeding bird. As soon as a likely victim was spotted, the game-cock would be taken out of his basket, his spurs tied on, and finally he would be put down as close to the other as possible. Pheasants are naturally belligerent. It would not be long before the issue was joined; though of course it could never have been long in doubt what the eventual outcome would be. The wild bird would have little chance against the trained and practised fighter. But armed in addition as the latter was with those long, slim, murderous spurs. . . .

Still, it was a better way than shooting them out of trees.

The old bloodstock traits come out strongly in Kit. The sheep he herds are thoroughbreds. It is as much a hobby as a livelihood with him; though, in all conscience, in such matters he has his head screwed on all right. There will no one get the better of him in a deal: they will do remarkably well, I think, if they hold their own. I know I couldn't. I am sure that, almost before he spoke, what business sense I had would be all charmed away.

Such is Kit Metcalfe, gentleman.

Who is there left? I am dodging about my valley

like a magpie, instead of starting at the top and working down.

There is John Bracken: one cannot overlook *him*, for I should think he must stand six feet six. A huge and powerful, slow-moving man with tremendous muscles and a perpetual smile. A splendid farmer; teetotal; and as good-natured as one could wish. In any time of trouble everybody calls upon John Bracken. He himself, and all he has, is at the service of anyone who asks. He is a cheerful, contented man, happy in his wife and home and family. All three are good. The house he lives in never seems to need repair. His wife is as bonny and as young-looking as when he wed her twenty years ago; and all his children—I think there are seven of them— are well and strong and fairly-grown.

I like John Bracken, though he does keep in the background. Only once, I think, has he loomed in the public eye. That was in Badgerley, and I was there. A bull got loose and ran amok; scared no doubt by the noisy throng which surged that market day along the High Street. Things looked ugly for a moment; when through the screaming, shouting throng, there came the huge form of John Bracken. He strode across the clear space the bull had made and grasped a horn. A quick jerk and he had hold of both; standing fairly and squarely straight in front of the maddened beast. Then we, we others standing back from that clear-spaced arena where man and beast were isolated, saw his strength. Over to one side he forced that massive neck, twisting the madly snorting head beneath his hands. Over, over: further, further. The fore knees bent; the great body swayed unsteadily, trying to recover. But that pressure was inexorable. Over at last went the huge body with a crash. It lay there still.

Typical of Bracken, too, it was, that he would allow nobody to put the new chain through its nose ring but himself. He waved us back and, as the bull rose to its feet again, he gentled it, speaking calmly to it all the while. Fear in the poor beast died away. Two or three minutes afterwards it was being guided quietly and easily along the street. Bracken laughed, in his own kindly way, at the congratulations showered upon him. He dusted his great hands, one with the other, and rejoined his wife in the grocer's shop.

A quiet, peace-loving man. It is as well. I should not care to meet him angry.

But then, there is no chance of that. No one is ever angry in my valley. How can they be?

Chapter XXII

Consummation

*

And now we finish. I have told you all I know. To your imagination only will I leave the thoughts of what delight I find in my river now; how many things I find to see and do upon its banks; and how I have made it all a garden of wild flowers so that, at times, I do not fish at all. Nor will I tell you further how I share it, and with whom; and how, even to the end, I have contrived to keep its child-like laughter unimpaired. I have not forgotten. My river can still bring joy and happiness to any child. I am glad of it; for I realize now, as perhaps I have never fully done before, that— among fishermen at least—the child is undoubtedly true father of the man.

My hatchery has thrived. Now, at last, I have the beautiful glass grilles that I had hungered for. Each May I turn in many thousand fry, for by then there is food and to spare for all of them. Every inch of water in my valley, I should think, now sends its quota down to the streams. The streams themselves have altered beyond all knowing. When first I came, in the whole valley there would not be half a mile of water where it was possible to fish. Now, with the dams and groins I have thrown across, there are nearer ten. Good fishing too. Away up even in the fells I can see results. My fish are larger, more numerous; they come into order sooner; they fight harder, more powerfully; they are better in every way. Gone are the lean years for them. Now there is always food, and shelter too: the floods which devastated their haunts have, for them at least, lost half their terrors. They hide behind my groins, or in some quieter corner of the pools. There are plenty of places now to go to when the storm-water comes lashing down in fury from the hills.

And my lake—what should I say about my lake? It lies there like a jewel throned; so calm, so peaceful, so exquisitely lovely that I often lose all desire to fish. I sit down as I reach it, my rod and flies neglected, and I lie there looking at it until it is time for me to go back home.

But there are fish in it—whoppers. The trout must have soon found their way in from the river, and they must have gorged continually on the mass of insect life washed off the newly flooded herbage. I realized in time that this supply would not last for ever, and I took advice on planting. Lakewort I introduced; lakewort in quantity. It grew amazingly; and round the sides I planted irises and lilies—a host of water plants which delighted me to look upon, apart entirely from any value they might hold as fly-farms for the fish.

As a matter of fact it was quite a long time before I realized that fish were in my lake at all; for seldom, during that first year, even on the calmest nights, when the moths were fluttering about in droves, was there any sign of a rise. I might hear a "plop" somewhere over by the islands, and the rings would ripple slowly across towards me, but it was exceptional. And yet, I thought, there must be fish there, surely! It was such a glorious stretch of water, and I had engineered the entrance so that the level was maintained and a way-in left for any trout to go who wished. Some of course, I suppose, *did* go; but I imagined that they, those first pioneers, would have in any case turned bottom feeders.

However, thought I, I will alter that in time.

I stocked with fry the next spring, and the next, and the next after that. They would grow quickly, I hoped, those fry. But I was disappointed. For three seasons very little showed. There would be a bit of a rise, some summer nights; but nothing to what I had expected. Those thousands of fry I had put in must have all been eaten; or died; or—a grim thought, this—they had all followed the example of their predecessors and were feeding only on the bottom. I studied the matter very thoroughly, and then I gave it up. I was content not to fish there, anyway. The place lost none of its loveliness for me. Still, I worried a good deal, I must admit.

Then one day, in a little fishing pub away over in the wilds of Galway, I found out all about it. In one of the public rooms which I occasionally frequented, I found a month-old copy of the *Fishing Gazette*. I glanced through it interestedly, for somehow I had missed seeing this number before; and there, in the correspondence column, I found just what I wished to know. Someone had suffered even as I had done. And he had bought ants' eggs and cast them upon the waters of his lake so that the wind would carry them across. They had floated on the surface, well spread out, and the fish had gone for them bald-headed. He had taught his trout to rise!

Just what I wanted! I cut my stay short—the trout were not rising there, either—and I bought a lot of ants' eggs. They weigh very light: there are a great number of them in a pound.

Consummation

And then I too, with the wind behind me, scattered my largesse abroad.

For the first twenty or thirty yards, as the eggs drifted out, there was nothing stirred. And then I suddenly caught the flash of a great golden body as it turned and broke the surface. Then another, and another, and another. In a moment, it seemed, all about that spot was alive with fish—it boiled. It was amazing. There was a strong ripple and I must have missed seeing scores and scores of rises. But I saw enough; I saw enough.

I ran along the bank, throwing handfuls of ants' eggs high into the air so that they would blow well out on to the water. I ran a furlong or more; and as I looked back, all along that length and now spreading farther and farther out towards the middle were the rings of rising fish. It was astounding. All the way across they rose. I saw breaks, scores of them, far out among the bigger waves long after the stampede had quietened down nearer the shore. The eggs were drifting across and the new fish were finding them.

I recaptured youth that afternoon. I laughed and chuckled like a sandboy. Why, my lake must be full of trout; full!

I wrote out an order for more ants' eggs that night. I overdid it, thoroughly. I used far too many;

for, later on, when I walked round there, I found great numbers washed up on the opposite shore. Still, I learnt sense in time. I soon got to know just the right quantity to put in to bring the trout up and keep them busy for a while.

And then, with this, there came quite suddenly the realization of the weapon which had been put into mine hand. Those experts . . . those know-all fellows who had laughed at me—me and my dams; those super-efficient devils who had all stared down their noses at me when I mentioned fishing and then forgot me and went on talking about "pig"! What could I not do to those?

I made myself perfect. I got so that I could bring on a rise at any time I wished. It was quite remarkable; especially so at this early season of the year when, in the nature of things, there was not a great deal of fly about and the fish kept down more even than they usually did. I planned out everything. No general ever gave more careful, studied thought to the ordering of his campaign.

And then I sent off my invitations. Just three of them—rather attractive invitations; subtly flattering; subtly enticing. "Lake flies," I mentioned. . . . "I had a lake. . . ."

They came. All three. I fetched them on from Furrowfield late one afternoon.

Consummation

After dinner I opened my campaign. I led them on gently at first—gently—gently—oh, it was good to feel such power in my hands—and soon I had them in their condescending mood; just where I wanted them. I pretended to glance at the weather. "Better start tomorrow morning at about nine o'clock," I suggested, airily. "There should be a rise on then. Don't you think so?" I turned to the one I detested most.

He blew a cloud of cigar smoke up towards the ceiling and watched it curl slowly away. His head rested on the back of his chair. He never even glanced towards me. "No, I *don't*," he replied, at last. There was no mistaking it; he didn't!

"Well, what time would *you* suggest then?"

"Eleven o'clock is early enough this weather," he asserted. "We may get a fish or two between then and, say, two o'clock." He blew another cloud up heavenwards and frowned portentously. "Personally speaking," he drawled, "I should doubt if there will be a rise at all." He broke off petulantly, flicking off his ash and looking both bored and annoyed. "I wish you had mentioned it was so cold up here."

I left him for a moment. "What do you fellows think?" I asked, turning to the others.

Apparently they were unanimous. They replied

offhandedly, as though the question were superfluous. "Oh, Derek's right!" they agreed. "There'll be nothing doing until towards midday. The water's cold yet, you know." They stated the fact in the same patient, explanatory tone they would have used to a child. Superiority complex, I suppose.

"Well, I think you're all wrong," I answered truculently—well, truculently for me. "There'll be a rise at nine o'clock and another at ten. And as for your eleven to two theory, I don't hold with it at all. I think they'll go off until about three."

They glanced at each other and smiled.

I gabbled on. I grew quite dogmatic, even as they. I knew, of course, that they were right. That was why I hated them so much. They were always right. But that was speaking generally; out of their vast knowledge. They didn't know what I knew about *my* trout. And so I, in this my hour, went on to argue belligerently about their rods, their flies, their method of fishing lakes. All that they said I disagreed with. I got my own back that evening for all that they had done and said and—what I hated worse—implied when they had been up before. I burnt my boats completely. I was committed for the morning following. *Vae victis!*

I went in to see George before I went to bed. I

told him what I wanted; and of course he, as usual, understood. He and three lads, well-hidden out of sight behind the high bank of the ghyll bordering the lake, and beneath which, on the twenty-yards strip of shore there was between it and the water, we should be fishing. He and three lads and some ants' eggs.

"T' wind will be just reight," he informed me. "At nine and ten, and then again at three and four. I'll nooan forget."

I gave him a pound of ants' eggs. "A few at a time, George," I said. "well up in the air, so that we can't see them. Keep yourselves out of sight."

I pressed those three, the following morning, to take their rods with them. It was barely half-past eight, and there was just nice time to get their tackle ready and be at the lake by nine. But they would have none of it. Their knowledge and experience told them "No". It was a cold, grey morning; and in normal circumstances, and on any normal lake, there would, I knew myself, be nothing doing. But I pressed them hard—it was part of my plan—and though they would not trouble about their rods, they did it last consent to walk down with me to see.

We got there at five minutes to nine. A good breeze was blowing straight across from where we stood on the strip of shore under the shelter of the high and wooded bank which hid the ghyll. The water looked dead, with leaden-coloured wavelets monotonously following one another. There was not a sign of anything alive over all its length.

Derek laughed. He ostentatiously drew out his watch and glanced at it. "Did you mention a rise?" he asked. "Nine o'clock, I think you. . . ."

He was interrupted by a resounding splash about twenty yards out. I believe that for a moment he thought one of us had flung a stone in. But he was quickly disillusioned. The rise came on. In half a minute there were fish jumping and splashing all along a belt running parallel with the shore and anything from twenty to fifty yards in depth. And then farther out still. Even as we watched, the rise extended. New fish came on the feed. We could see the dark backs breaking the surface in lovely head and tail rises, while every now and then a really big fellow would leap clear and fall back with a re-sounding whack. It was a spectacular show. I en-joyed it.

"Strange!" muttered Derek, after about five minutes of it. "I suppose there must be a hatch of some sort on—iron-blues, most likely."

I laughed quietly to myself. Iron-blues!

Consummation

"Nine o'clock," I said, casually. "There'll be another rise at about ten. . . ."

"Twelve, I think," commented Derek. "Feed about every three hours, trout. At least *I*'ve found it so." The supercilious emphasis on the "I" maddened me anew.

"I'd advise ten," I said, shortly, as we turned about to go home.

I think they were a little, a very little, more amenable to suggestion as time progressed. "We might as well go down," said one. "After all, there may be odd ones rising through the morning." It was a grudging admission, but it sufficed. They got out their tackle.

I commented adversely on their flies. I hated doing it, for they were lovely things, and I knew that, on any lake but mine, they would kill fish. They ought, of course, to do so on mine; but I knew they wouldn't.

My suggestions fell on deaf ears, however. I showed them half a dozen tiny spider hackles— imitation nymphs, like we use on the river. "These are what you want," I said. "Let me give you some."

They examined them disinterestedly; passing them one to another without comment; with hardly a glance as a matter of fact.

"Won't try them, eh?" I grinned. "All right."

George started the performance dead on time. I had just got my victims nicely separated and myself a hundred yards or so beyond the farthest of them when the fun began. I saw the rise commence and then ripple all along the line. I had three tiny midge flies on—the ones I had shown them—and on the point of each I fixed a couple of ants' eggs. It was dirty work; very dirty. My morals had gone. I had jettisoned every spark of feeling towards these three. I was out for their scalps.

And I got them!

I had rises almost every cast, and I hooked my fish good and hard. I did not mean to lose any. By the time the main rise was over I had a dozen. I fished on a while and managed to pick up another two. Then I walked down towards those others. One of them had got a brace; the others nothing.

"We may as well go home now," I said. "There'll be nothing more until the middle of the afternoon."

I think they listened to what I had to say now with more respect. They wavered. I could see them doing it. The sight of those fourteen fish against their two, coming as it did on top of my accurate forecast of those absurdly timed rises, had rather shaken their aplomb. But the experience of years still held. No; they would stay and fish on.

"Right-o," I assented, blithely. "I'll have some sandwiches sent down. I have some work to do. I'll be back again about three o'clock."

I overtook George on the way home. He was going to fill in the intervening time in the garden. I congratulated him heartily. Never a sign had we seen of either him or any of his accomplices. The ants' eggs of course, thrown high into the air, had to us been totally invisible.

At about half-past two I joined them again. Of course they had done nothing. There had been no rise to mean anything ever since the time I had left them four hours or so before. All three appeared to be considerably subdued. For half an hour I yarned away with them; and then, casting my eyes towards the sky, I casually remarked: "Well, they should be coming on again about now, don't you think?"

I got no answer. They took my word for it and separated.

Again George did his work magnificently. And again did I do mine. I got seven or eight on that occasion, whereas they failed entirely. And this time, when I rejoined them, they fairly hung upon my words. Derek examined the cast that I had on —of course all trace of egg had been removed— and muttered something to himself. The others were even more impressed.

"Four o'clock, you say the next rise is likely?"

"Yes," I remarked, looking wise. "I think they will come on again about four."

And then I added a very silly remark. My triumphs had gone to my head. "You had better try a cast of these flies," I said.

It was certainly a bitter pill for them to swallow; those colossal, self-opinionated experts. They hated it; but one of them was beaten. He pocketed his pride and said he would.

I could have kicked myself. I couldn't give *him* ants' eggs! And there was no possible doubt whatever that he was a better fisherman than I in every way. If I got fish and he didn't, he would guess that there was something very wrong somewhere. Still, I was committed now. I made him up a cast identical with mine: spring-black; waterhen; light and dark snipes—little hackled river flies.

The others started fishing, but we two sat and smoked a while. And then, a few minutes before zero hour, we took up our positions.

The rise, desultory at first, soon grew. It was not so good as those others, I am glad to say; but it brought me the biggest triumph of the day. I say the biggest, because I earned it honestly. My neighbour with the nymph flies got half a dozen—one more than I did, in spite of my ants' eggs. Half a dozen really good fish. It looked as though I had dropped on the first moment of all those years for a cast of flies to work. I had taught those fish to come to the top, and now—for the first time, so far as I was aware—they had looked for other food besides ants' eggs. The one moment. And the flies I had chosen; the little wet-fly hackles; were the right ones; the natural ones the fish expected. My triumph was complete; for those others, fishing bigger, more fancy flies, had just flogged the water for an hour in vain.

That night they *listened* when I spoke. There were no more clouds of cigar smoke blown towards the ceiling when I made a statement. I was one of the élite.

That spring was the turning point in my lake. Perhaps it was the ants' eggs; perhaps it was the gradual exhaustion of the bottom feed; but whatever the cause, the fish rose well all through that summer. As the season advanced the hatch of fly was very large—I had several boards down in odd corners, and of course the waterside plants were used as well—and, once started, the allure of this new food proved irresistible. Confirmed bottom-feeders there still would be of course; but these, I thought, were probably the older fish who had

come in at first. I would have to try to get them
out with minnow. The fry I had put in two or
three years before had thrived tremendously. They
were heavy fish now; big, deep-backed, gloriously-
coloured trout who fought like tigers. Their average weight all through was vastly greater than that
of their confrères in the river; though there too, the
fish had improved in size beyond my wildest hopes.
There was little change—I had been careful of that
—in the actual character of my stream; but there
was a big alteration in that of its inhabitants.

And yet, after all, I had done very little. A few
dams thrown across; an odd obstruction placed
here and there; some plants transferred from one
place to another—that was about all. My hatchery
was a toy which amused me greatly; but a few
hours work and some wire-netting had, I am sure,
helped the restocking almost as much. Some of the
side streams were almost choked with naturally
hatched fry; fit little beggars who made their way
down to the river on their own and without any
help at all from me. The food supply was self-
supporting. I utilized, as I have said, every available
bit of water where cress or marigolds or river-moss
would grow, and just left it to itself. Fly-boards
were no trouble, either; apart from an odd coat of

Consummation

bitumen now and then. They, too, looked after themselves. And as for the old gravel-beds my pools had covered—why, they were alive! I had no worries there! I never saw so many stone-flies in my life.

No; come to think of it, I have done but very little. Even my gardening efforts, in retrospect, seem infinitely small.

But how am I to tell you how dear my river is to me now? It is, at last, the stream that I had dreamed about; the river as I had seen it with the magic eyes of youth. More beautiful, I think, even than that. My little stream, singing the angler's song; slipping away through its trees and flowers . . . over the boulders. . . .

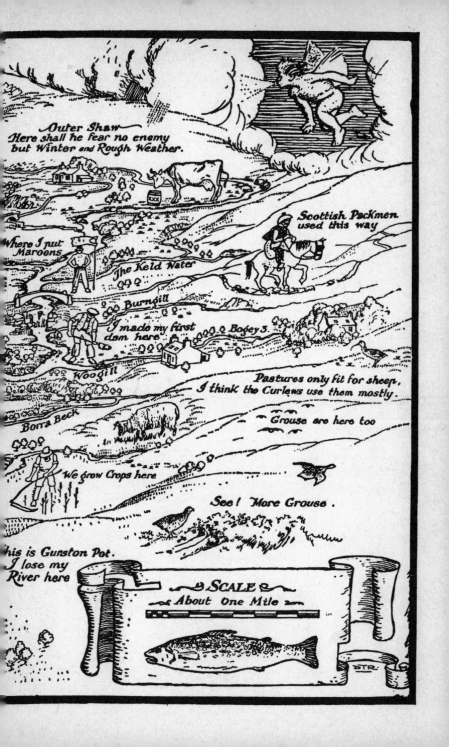